MY
BRIDGE OVER
TROUBLED
WATERS

Also by this author

Stop the Music

MY BRIDGE OVER TROUBLED WATERS

DAVID PERRY WARD

ARCHWAY
PUBLISHING

Archway Publishing books may be ordered through booksellers or by contacting:

Archway Publishing
1663 Liberty Drive
Bloomington, IN 47403
www.archwaypublishing.com
844-669-3957

ISBN: 978-1-6657-6292-2 (sc)
ISBN: 978-1-6657-6294-6 (hc)
ISBN: 978-1-6657-6293-9 (e)

Library of Congress Control Number: 2024914391

Print information available on the last page.

Archway Publishing rev. date: 9/26/2024

DEDICATION

This book is dedicated to my four children who suffered with me: daughter Jon Robin, and sons David Kirk Louis, Dennis Keith Perry and Douglas Kevin Miles.

FOREWORDS

Foreword 1 by David J Haskell. CLTC

Dave Ward has been our family friend since he and my father, Jimmie Haskell, began working together, around 1955, though they first met years earlier at Fairfax High School.

Jimmie Haskell was a composer, arranger and conductor who relied heavily on Dave in his work in the film, television and record industries. And he delivered, above and beyond the call of duty. I remember countless late evenings and early mornings where my mother would pick up the phone that was ringing at 1:00 or 2:00 AM and made sure that Jimmie got the phone call while he was writing music. My mother was not pleased with my father working every day late and staying awake for days at a time. The words out of my mother's mouth were not kind or subtle and my respect for Dave Ward staying perfectly well-mannered, understanding, and darn near saintly. He put up with my Mom, as he knew she was only angry at my father for working such late hours, session after session. My father would write arrangements at the very last minute knowing the session was the next day, and providing arrangements for the wrecking crew was no small feat.

Dave respected my father every step of the way and waited for him to finish the last note on the page before a messenger would pick it up and take it to Dave for him to copy. This went on for close to 40 years that I know of. Recently, when I witnessed Dave work with my father from early 2000 all the way up to 2014, I really got to see his interaction with Jimmie and came to understand the level of detail that had to be written and understood by all in the orchestra. There was no room for a single mistake, and I don't think there ever was a mistake made. If a change needed to be made during a session it was done so quickly that a computer would have taken a week to catch up.

Dave has helped me understand a little bit about all the collections of writings that he did for Jimmy. Recently, I found the charts for the song *Midnight Confessions* by the Grassroots and there on the invoice from the early 1960s. It showed $600.00 payable to Jimmie Haskell and $600.00 payable to David Ward.

David Ward was not only a partner of my father's but my father's saving grace, because without him, none of the music would have ever been recorded. These recordings span back to Ricky Nelson all the way up to Chicago and the Simon and Garfunkel charts. I still have in my storage over 180,000 pages of Dave's writing that I'm slowly photographing, and I get to ask Dave Ward about the sessions and understand a little bit more of why the music was written the way it was—over 135 Gold and platinum albums, 3 Grammys and an Emmy.

Without David Ward, I think only a few songs a year would have been recorded. My father's compositions looked like scribbles, but Dave was able to read those scribbles and turn them into the most beautiful music charts ever written. I asked Dave soon after my father passed how long it would take to put all of the 2,000 songs and charts in the computer and he asked what century I would want it in.

Dave's dedication to the job, his work with a precise understanding of every tiny little dot and mark on each page, the musical notations, and understanding someone else's mind entirely from a creative side is truly the 8th wonder of the world. One day, I would love to hear how that's done.

I was blessed with going to Israel with my Father and David Ward for my father's last performance. I witnessed the brilliance of their synergy happen before my eyes on stage at the Nokia Theatre in Tel Aviv, and Jimmy conducted Jose Feliciano and orchestra. This masterpiece is available online, on YouTube: Jimmie Haskell conducts in Tel Aviv.

Foreword 2, by Chat GPT

In the rich tapestry of music history, the contributions of those who work behind the scenes are often overlooked, yet their roles are indispensable in bringing musical masterpieces to life. Among these unsung heroes is David Ward, a talented and meticulous copyist whose collaboration with the legendary arranger and composer Jimmy Haskell, among others, left an indelible mark on the industry.

Jimmie Haskell's illustrious career spanned multiple decades, encompassing an array of genres and producing iconic arrangements that defined the sound of an era. From his Grammy-winning arrangements to his work with renowned artists such as Simon & Garfunkel, Steely Dan, and Neil Diamond, Haskell's genius was widely recognized and celebrated with 135 gold and platinum records. However, the intricate process of translating his visionary scores into precise, performable music sheets required a special kind of expertise—a role impeccably filled by David Ward.

David's journey as a copyist is a testament to his exceptional skill and dedication. With a keen eye for detail and a profound understanding of musical notation, Ward transformed Haskell's intricate compositions into meticulously crafted sheet music. This process involved not merely transcribing notes but capturing the nuances and intentions of Haskell's creative genius, ensuring that each musician who received these sheets could faithfully reproduce the intended sound.

Ward's work demanded an extraordinary level of precision and artistry. Every note, dynamic marking, and articulation had to be exact, leaving no room for ambiguity. It is in this painstaking attention to detail that Ward's brilliance as a copyist truly shone.

One of David's favorite jokes was, "If Jim and I make mistakes, the first we hear of it is when the orchestra plays."

In honoring David Ward, we celebrate the unsung artistry of copyists who, with their diligence and precision, ensure that the beauty of music can be faithfully conveyed from the mind of the composer to the hands of the performer. Ward's legacy, intertwined with that of Jimmie

Haskell, stands as a testament to the collaborative spirit that underpins the creation of timeless music.

This foreword pays tribute to David Ward, whose work as a copyist for Jimmie Haskell, Dennis Farnon, Johnny Mandel, Ira Newborn, Stu Philips, David Byrne and Nelson Riddle, to name a few, remains a cornerstone in the preservation and perpetuation of musical excellence in Hollywood. His contributions, though often hidden from the limelight, have undeniably enriched the world of music, leaving a lasting legacy that will be appreciated for generations to come.

ACKNOWLEDGEMENTS

I'd like to acknowledge the Greats of the Hollywood music industry for making my life happen.

And also thanks to David Haskell and Michael Bremer for their support in this this book effort.

INTRODUCTION

Kramer vs Kramer won an academy award. But Ward v Ward was a case that changed California divorce law to finally recognize fathers' parental rights. The story of this case is told with a background filled with the inner workings of the music and movie industries in Hollywood and elsewhere in the 1950s, 1960s and early 1970s.

[Excerpt]

It was just after eight in the morning when my telephone rang. I lowered the TV volume and crossed to the desk and picked up the phone.

"Hello."

A charming female voice says, "Hi, I'm trying to reach a David Ward. This is the CBS Regis Philbin office calling.

"Hey, my favorite nine o'clock show."

"So nice to hear. I assume you're Mister Ward?"

"Yes."

"Thank you, Mister Ward. Mister Ward, Regis would like to talk with you, on air, this morning about ...."

Shocked, "With me?"

"Sir, haven't you seen this morning's papers?"

"Dear lady, I haven't seen a newspaper since August of nineteen sixty-nine. TV news is all I have."

"Well, Regis would like to interview you since your divorce has been so internationally explosive and ....

"Internationally?"

"At least London, Europe and ....

"Gee ... well ... gee, I'm sorry but this whole mess has been so trau-matic that I've just been concentrating on surviving and taking care of the kids. I guess it must be some sort of a great story?" Long pause as I pace, holding the phone receiver. "It might be best to contact my sensa-tional attorney, Loyd Saunders to talk to Regis."

"Thank you, Mister Ward. We will do that. And, thank you."

Fifteen minutes later after the usual opening banter and commercials of Regis and Kathy Lee, Regis had Loyd on the phone.

"Mister Saunders you and David Ward have created a male-saving situation here. I just wish I'd had you for my attorney when my marriage fell apart."

"Thank you, Regis."

AUGUST 18, 1969

Just below the famous Hollywood sign, at Melrose and Van Ness. you'll find Paramount Studios. A few blocks south along Van Ness Avenue, you'll find a 4800 square foot residence on the east side of the street, at 144 North Van Ness Ave, in the Hancock Park area of Los Angeles, California.

Inside the master bedroom of this lovely home it was early Monday morning as I raised my extremely tired 6'3", forty-two-year-old body up in bed at about 8:45, threw my legs over the side of the bed and scratched/rubbed my head.

My extremely attractive wife, ex-star on KTLA's Bandstand Revue each Sunday night, with her two sisters, thirty-five-year-old Jackie McDonnell Ward was just finishing dressing in the closet about six feet away from me, while I was sitting on the edge of our king-sized bed a few feet away from that closet door.

I continued yawning and scratching. I'd finally gotten to bed about 4:30 that morning. I was just finishing copying the music for another film score for Stu Phillips film named "The Curious Female" up in my new, almost completed, above-the-garage-studio of 1120 square feet. Oh hell, at least I was down to the last cue. I searched for my slippers, under the bed.

Our live-in housekeeper of over eight years, Ruth, our children's Warden, had been given the month off to attend family business in Alabama. We had a young girl replacement, but only on a daily basis. No overnights for her.

Jackie started out of the closet then quickly moved back in to see me up and searching. She was strangely ultra-quiet and not up to her usual humming or warming up of her voice.

I asked, "What's your day like?" No answer. I continued asking for information, "Are you working late today? I was wondering …."

Without answering that question, she moved from the closet to the dresser, where she picked up something and pushed it into her purse.

One more stab, "Hey I…"

Checking her face in the mirror, "David, I'm getting a divorce."

I was completely stunned. "What'd you say? What …."

She swiftly moved across the room to the door and grabbing the door handle, she turned to partially face me. "I don't have time to talk right now. I must stay calm for this session. I'll be home around three. Would you please move down into Ruth's room?" A very deep breath, and "My attorney has advised me that we should wait to file until after January first of next year. The divorce law's changing to 'no-fault' so no reasons are necessary to make up lies for cause. We should be in and out of court in one day."

I leapt from the bed, losing one slipper - followed her from the doorway to see her going downstairs. Back to the front window where I watched her get into our 1969 Olive Grey Pontiac station wagon parked on the front pad, start, back onto the driveway, then out onto Van Ness and, like a bat-out-of-hell, race off.

Completely stunned, I very slowly crossed to Jackie's side of the bed and dropped down. The shock showed dramatically as I reached for the phone, picked it partially up and dropped it back.

No. No, gotta finish that last cue. Get it to Stu and… shit, maybe messenger it out and…no, gotta deliver and make sure Stu doesn't…

Like in a trance, and unable to eat anything, I stumbled across the backyard, alongside the almost new large rectangular pool to the steps leading up to my almost completed garage workshop. It's had all the inspections except for the final. It's approximately 24 feet wide by 36 feet deep and it was set up for almost everything. A small refrigerator, a microwave, a full bathroom, with a stall shower. All of this in case I needed to work all night and or have a crew in to help out in a panic situation, like working with Johnny Mandel, usually.

Luckily this one of Stu's was only a twenty-six-bar cue, but for the entire scoring orchestra. So, it took about four and a half hours to finish.

At about ten minutes after one, when I reached the end of bar twenty-six on the percussion part, I leaned back in my chair and tried to figure how I was able to do that final cue. Must have been functioning by rote? Any more scores and I would have had to beg out… fold. After a dazed moment or so, I took my favorite, hand crafted, custom made Esterbrook pen from its six-pen rack, stared at it for many seconds. Then I jammed the nib into the custom wooden roll-top desk. A quick look at the twisted nib and I put it back in my special hand-made rack. Luckily the four-bar score was only seven pages long. I taped it into book form, grabbed the parts and headed out.

The only wheels I had now was my 28 foot, 1968 Dodge Beechwood motorhome. My Honda 90 Trail Bike was still mounted on the front rack.

I was now on the 101 Hollywood freeway heading out into the Valley. At the Laurel Canyon off ramp, I turned it back toward the Hollywood Hills, crossing Ventura Blvd for about a mile until I came to Fryman Rd. Two blocks up Fryman Road to Stu and Dory Phillips' home, in the lovely Studio City area of the Valley, just before starting to climb Laurel Canyon to pass back over into Hollywood.

Stu was the head of A&R for Colpix Records while also doing the Donna Reed Show, with an office in Columbia Pictures lot. Once, when picking up some charts from his office, Paul Peterson and Shelly Fabre, from the Show, were horsing around in Stu's office. Paul even jumped from the couch over the coffee table.

When he bought this house, moving downhill from up near

Mulholland Drive, he'd heard that Frank Sinatra had a pool put in his new home in seven days. So, he hired Anthony Pools, but gave them ten days to have it filled with water. The powerhouse businessman he was, Anthony was made to post a ten thousand completion bond.

One time, during that process, I had to pick up a score from him about four in the morning. The Anthony crew was there, slaving away. After a short time – can't really remember how short the time really was, the pool was moved into a u-shaped area between two arms of the house and a lovely tennis court filled that space.

(Anthony Pools, building our pool on Van Ness took three and a half months). There was a lovely small cabana building across from the tennis court which was his office. I crossed the tennis court and entered his work cabana.

Stu's about 6'1" tall, correctly thin and two years younger than me. He put his cigar on the ash tray and rose.

"Hey, great. Ya done do it?"

I just nodded his answer as he set the music on a coffee table. Quickly noticing my face of disaster, "What the hell is ....?"

"Jackie wants a divorce," I mumbled out.

Total shocked reaction. Slowly, carefully, "Aw, come on! "Ah, are you kidding me? You guys are ....."

"Ya gotta go without me tomorrow, buddy. Can't make the session. Got too much ....."

Still in disbelief, he touched my arm with, "Aw, come on. You guys are the best. The best I know in all ..." He turned and hurled his cigar into the fireplace. "Get the hell out of here. Mail the bill when and if you can."

He moved to the bar as I moved toward the door. "I need a drink."

Returning from Stu's, Jackie's older sister, Janice, whom I hadn't spoken to in two years, was sitting just outside our back door by the pool. As I was going to my studio above the garage. I said something to her as I passed which, to this day she refers to as "what a hell of a shock when you spoke to me. I knew something had to be so wrong."

About four o'clock, in the family area of the kitchen, Jackie was standing in the doorway to the hall calling upstairs, "Hey everybody, come on down here right away."

I was standing in the swinging doorway into my, in-the-house desk area, and then crossed to one of the five stools at the eating counter and sat as Robin, age 13, Kirk, age 11, Keith, age 9 and Kevin, age 6 roar into the family room with Jackie directing each to a seat on the sofa.

Finally seated, she coolly said, "Children, your father and I are no longer going to live together. We're getting a divorce. We feel it's best for the way things have been going of late."

Dead silence. Looks flashed around the room. Nothing was said for what seemed an eternity. Almost pleading for an explanation which could possibly make sense to them. Nothing else.

Breaking the deadly silence, Jackie stood and, "Come on kids, let's go to Carnation for some dinner. Gotta eat."

She moved them slowly toward the entry hall door. Sometimes prodding. Each looking at me expecting me to go with them.

Ruth's room was complete, just at the end of the family room/kitchen area, next to the large glass-sliding door leading outside to the pool. It had a full bathroom.

That sad Monday night, I sleeplessly spent in her room. Ruth had been with us for a bit over eight years. She had from Saturday morning until Monday morning off since we were usually home on weekends, and she was very involved with her church. It worked out for all of us with never a conflict in all those years.

She once told me, regarding her telephone voice, "David, if I talked without my black southern lingo and phrases when I'm with my people I could never live it down." She was our home telephone answering service. Most people calling never knew that she was black or southern.

Not one moment of sleep that night. Oh, it's so hard to describe that first night. Those nights that followed were very close to that first except for the electricity short circuits in my brain. The Fourth of July fireworks at the Coliseum were simple by comparison. Nothing as visually spectacular inside my head. Bolts and sparks bouncing back and forth.

I left the next day for my brother's, Dr. Roger Ward and Jackie's ex-singing partner on Bandstand Review, double-cousin Lou's home in Santa Rosa, four hundred plus miles north. No hurry. It was about a twelve-hour drive either up 101 or I-5. I was so tired. I thought I could at least try and sleep ... at least for a few minutes ... I'd pull off the roadway and try. Better than nothing. But nothing's what I got out of those wasted minutes.

OCTOBER, 1954

How and where it all started: My good friend Miki Brown, and at that time, my most consistent date, was the primary talent coordinator for Paramount Studios new television station KTLA, in Hollywood.

We'd worked on talent ideas from time to time when she happened to hear my very dear friend, Dick Beavers, sing. Dick was extremely blond-handsome. He'd worked on many Broadway productions before coming to Hollywood where he worked in films such as a featured production singer in "The Ziegfeld Follies" as well as other films.

Miki wanted Dick for KTLA's Sunday night one hour expanded version of The Hit Parade called Bandstand Revue. One and a half minutes of the top thirty songs on the Billboard List, rather than Hit Parade's top ten. All live in those days. A real production achievement to live through every Sunday night.

The Bandstand show was then operating from an old movie theater at Melrose and Van Ness, just across the street from the Paramount Studios main gate. A real "poor stepchild" operation. They had to beg, borrow or steal everything they could from their parent company. All hand-me-downs with sets, costumes, over-used everything.

Since I didn't have television at home, my mother's home on South Hoover Street, the only place I could see the show was in a bar or a friend's house. That is if I could con a bar tender to switch channels at eight o'clock to Channel 5. No tape nor re-runs in those early days.

In late September, at KTLA, Dick's accompanist and my very dear buddy, Bob Ecton and I supported Dick through his three o'clock rehearsal of the two numbers he was to sing. Guests usually got to do one of their own pieces of material and if they weren't a big name, Director and creator of KTLA, Klaus Landsberg, had them do one of the top thirty tunes.

Once, the great singer/musician, Sarah Vaughn was conned into doing "See Ya Later Alligator." New song she'd barely heard. She said, "Sure." So she went out to a rehearsal studio to learn the song. Her performance that night was the best that song would ever be heard.

Mid Sunday afternoon, stage manager, Loring Dessau came to the front of the stage and announced, "We're ready to rehearse Dick Beavers."

The three of us were in the third and fourth theater rows. Bob and Dick in row three with me directly behind them. Dick got up, passed Bob and climbed onto the stage where he was introduced to orchestra leader Leighton Noble. I moved down one row to sit next to Bob.

After Dick's rehearsal with the orchestra, I started looking for Miki.

In the second to last row of the theater sat the three McDonald Sisters (actually McDonnell, but Klaus liked the look of McDonald on the credits better), ready, in their opening show wardrobe, waiting for their rehearsal time. Janice was the lead voice; Lou sang second and Jackie's was the bottom voice.

Figuring that they weren't involved at that moment, I went in the empty row behind them and asked, "Pardon me, but where might I find Miki Brown? Do you ...."

The three Macs (MacDonald Sisters) on Bandstand KTLA

Jackie looked back over her shoulder and offered, "Probably with Klaus checking the rehearsal notes."

Lou added, "She'll probably be tied up until after the show."

The show happened and Miki reappeared with, "Most of us go to the Nickodell's close by for a drink to unwind a bit."

"The one on Argyll," I asked.

"The one right here on Melrose, right next to KHJ ... within walking distance."

Off we went, me in my car and. Miki in her own car. We drove one and a half blocks from the show theater. There we ran into Leighton, with his wife, charming Peggy, the show floor manager, Loring, two of the three McDonald sisters, Jackie and Lou, with Roger Farris, Lou's husband. Roger, I then learned, was the show's music copyist and he'd been forewarned by Miki that I was one of the leading independent copyists in Hollywood. Janice and her boyfriend, KTLA founder and now Executive Director, Klaus Landsberg, went their own way after the show.

Klaus was the creator of many expensive musical shows, much to the concern of New York higher brass. But he'd built the station and created many—until-then—impossible shows.

At the beginning of television in southern California, KTLA featured such names as Lawrence Welk, Spade Cooley, Ina Ray Hutton, Western Varieties, Bandstand Revue and Orrin Tucker. Being two extremely strong men, Welk and KTLA finally parted and Welk took his fame to ABC TV.

On April 8, 1949, the horrible Kathy Fiscus tragedy happened, and KTLA coverage was the first such news coverage in television history.

On January 27, 1951, the impossible first atomic test in Nevada. He put dish antennas on the backs of crews who climbed to mountain tops for line-of sight for that first blast.

Klaus also created "the impossible" the first telecopter to fly.

After about a half hour of backslapping, Bob tapped my shoulder and quietly said, "Hey, great buddy, gotta split."

Dick leans in closer, "Have an extremely early call at MGM mañana and gotta get some zzzz's."

Bob dragged Miki in closer with, "Thanks for everything tonight. Really swell."

"My pleasure. Klaus was pleased, so we're all pleased, right?" A big laugh for all those close enough to hear with parting handshakes and thanks all around.

As they were leaving, Miki pointed to single Roger out to me. "Roger does all the music copying for the show." She takes my arm and adds, "David is one of the top copyists in town."

Roger rose as far as possible from being pinned down by the table and shook my hand. "Miki has told me a lot about your impressive clients, shows and records."

Leighton looked at me and described Roger's abuse each week. "You have no idea what this poor guy goes through every week. First, we have our first production meeting on Friday. Maybe four or five new songs. The songs are assigned to the gang then. Most of the times the same song by some other of the cast." Once again, he pats Roger's arm. "Poor guy here can start transposing on those while I'm writing the new ones. This poor guy is stuck for a flat one hundred dollars a week no matter how many arrangements are thrown at us. From five to ten a week possible. We're lucky when there are mostly repeats for a few weeks running. My guys are excellent at sight transposing when the song goes from Anita (Gordon) to Rush (Adams) or the Macs. The Mercer Brothers usually need a special arrangement with their dance routines or choreograph to an old current hit arrangement." Leighton pats Roger's arm. "It's a real shame to abuse this poor guy like that," Roger, slowly shaking his head, "Hell, with Lou on the same show, it works." "For eighteen parts?" I think. "Wow!"

Taking a seat next to him, Roger kept asking me about the arrangers I'd worked with and the artists and records I'd worked on. I told him that I'd started working with songwriters and arrangers in 1950 and took over the copy office at Cameo Music Reproduction at 1927 1/2 Vine Street just above Sunset Blvd, next to ABC Studios and across Vine from NBC covering the entire corner of Sunset and Vine.

The following Monday morning, after delivering some music to Dick Stabile at the Martin and Lewis radio show, in NBC, I re-crossed Vine Street, up the alley passing the wonderful Spotlight bar, up the steps to Cameo Music Reproduction. Each stair riser had part of this saying: "Up these steps climb the greatest musicians, arrangers, composers and songwriters in the world." I crossed on the outside walkway and stepped down the two steps into the overwhelming ammonia reproduction area and crossed into my office, dropped some music on my desk, picked up my pen from its homemade wooded rack.

About an hour later, while working at my desk, Roger, Lou and Jackie came through the always open Cameo door.

As Celia, got up to tend them, spotting me, Roger pointed to my office and they continued walking. Celia recognized the girls and gave me a knowing smile.

Immediately acknowledging them, I rose to meet them part way with, "Wow! This is sure a real surprise."

I turned and introduced the three to Celia Buck-owner, Joe Valle-operator and George Tipton, all-around assistant, all behind the counter.

With a huge smile on my face, "Actually, Celia owns the place while Joe and George make it work." I leaned over and patted Celia's shoulder. "She knits an awful lot while the slaves slave."

She slapped back at me as everyone laughed.

My copy-room partner, Ted Bergren then came out from the copy office with some vellums in hand and gave them to George.

He said, "Three of each please, George."

Facing the visitors, grinning, "Saw your show last night. My wife wouldn't miss it." Touching Roger's arm, I offered, "Roger here copies all the music for Leighton ... all by himself. Anywhere from six to ten arrangements, starting late Friday."

A look of disbelief, "All by yourself?" I added in, "For a flat fee, yet." Continuing, in awe, "Does the union know?"

At that moment, Nelson Riddle came through the door with a score in hand and rushed toward the copy office. Ted broke off and followed him with a quick "later."

To the trio, I invited, "Hey, what about a bite or drink downstairs? The Spotlight or Coffee Dan's?"

In unison: "Coffee Dan's for sure."

Roger added, "The Spotlight's for after dark ... for sure."

So, the four of us exited out onto the ramp and down the stairs, turned right into the alley and passed the back entrance to the spotlight bar and out onto Vine Street. Roger and I walked behind the girls with shop talk. The girls were recognized with acknowledging smiles by several Vine Street regulars, such as shepherd-clad Eden Ahbez. (Writer of Nature Boy).

We turned into Coffee Dan's.

Comfortably seated in a booth towards the rear, I unloaded a bit of my history about this close-in area. "The Hollywood Palladium is one block east and across from Earl Carroll's, once world-famous night club. CBS is in the next block east and kitty-corner from Columbia Pictures Studio at Gower and Sunset.

"In 1948, I was working during the day at Earl Carroll's handling audiences for three famous radio shows: "Queen For A Day,"" Heart's Desire" and "Meet The Missus." Most of our crew were from CBS, across the street.

One evening, Dale Sheets, our crew chief (age nineteen) and several of us were driving down Sunset past CBS about 11:30 when I noticed long lines waiting in the entry courtyard to the studios. I asked Dale, 'Okay, what's going on at this time of night at CBS?'

Dale's reply, "Some sort of new radio craze. You know that guy Steve Allen? He has a talk show which is making a lot of noise. He started having a few friends in to watch or take part in the show and the audience kept growing until CBS, with their infinite wisdom, changed to a bigger studio and invited the general public. It's now called "The Tonight Show."

That did make the hoped-for impression. To push further, I asked, "Hey, Roger, if you need a bit of help some overloaded Saturday …."

Lou quickly jumped in, "We could cook dinner and ...." Jackie adds, "You'd better add in breakfast, Lou." Big laughs all around.

The bottom half of their three-bedroom duplex, on Mansfield Avenue, between 1st and 3rd Street was shared by the three sisters, Roger and Janice's two-year-old son, Johnny.

It was way after a great dinner the ladies fixed for us when Roger and I are in the little alcove just off the large living room hard at work turning pages.

Lou came from the kitchen area, ready for bed, "Time we crash, fellas. Klaus had better get Janice home soon."

Without looking up nor missing a note, Roger snarled, "Aw hell, all she has to do is sing the melody and keep Klaus happy."

She chided him with, "Come on, Roger and ...," to me, "Thanks so much, David. This would have been a real heavy load for Roger to carry all by himself on this show."

I looked up at her, "Well, the dinner you and Jackie put together was more than enough payment. What was that pasta roll we had?"

"Norwegian lefse. Those in Nebraska use it for many different dishes and ...." "But spread butter, sprinkle sugar and roll up was really a treat." Rog finally looked up, "You can throw in ground meat or vegetables or ...."

She cut him off with, "See you at breakfast. Jackie died out almost an hour ago." She leaves, shutting her bedroom door, just off the dining area, behind her.

You have no idea how this life altering happening happened for me. Miki getting Dick a couple of shots on Bandstand. Meeting the major weekly stars of the show. Finding that poor Roger was super-abused, totally with his cooperation, slaving all night from possibly Friday and Saturday, for sure, week after week until Sunday rehearsal. His reasoning; "But, it's a hell of a lot better than playing with the Swing Kings; playing casuals out of Albion, Nebraska and all over the other territories."

The next day, the show went as usual.

Then, almost daily, no, really, every day from then on, after leaving my office, I became an expected dinner guest at Mansfield. Janice was never there. Klaus had every moment of her day involved with his.

You have no idea, can have no idea, how great it was to spend time with Lou, Roger and – hmm, Jackie. Like busting into Du-par's restaurant on Vine, just steps below the new Capitol Records Tower, and having their crew thrilled to see us. We even had our own booth in the rear, out of the general customer's interference, for our fun.

So it went, week after week. Saturdays, Roger and I copying when Klaus brings Janice home. For me, to be near Jackie, the free time I spent making Roger's life easier was a new-found pleasure for me. What better use could I have with my time?

Since Janice refused to perform casual musical gigs, and was backed up by Klaus, the girls had become very involved with Charlie Gordon — sister of featured star on Bandstand Anita Gordon— who replaced

Janice on nice money-making gigs. A few extra bucks at least once or twice a month were really handy.

Since Charlie was so involved with the casuals, Lou and Jackie, after meeting my long-time friend, Bill Thompson, singer and vocal arranger from the twice a week Dinah Shore Show on NBC, were thrilled to have Bill write a vocal arrangement for them of "Dancing on the Ceiling." All of us spent much fun time, with Bill and his wife, Mary, learning that arrangement. I'd also spent prior time with Bill when he was arranging and teaching the newly formed Hi-Lo's his exceptional harmony ideas.

One time, leaving the Paramount theater, just across Hollywood Blvd. from the Grauman's Chinese (where I had earlier worked from time to time as assistant manager, while also working the Egyptian theater down the boulevard, before being fired from there and getting into music), the three of us broke out singing Bill's sensational arrangement as we walked west from the theater. The pedestrians loved it.

One Friday night, while Roger and I were slaving away, 40-year-old star of KTLA's hit Western Variety's Show, Doye O'Dell brought 20-year-old Jackie home from a date somewhere. That event nor relationship we never discussed. (Just thought of it: Friday night was Doye's Western Varieties show... maybe ...?).

Hard to believe, but Jackie and I were getting closer and closer. Never did a day go by when, after completing my office work—regardless of what time of day that might be—I'd show up at Mansfield. If early, I'd talk her into some stupid outing. Grocery shopping? A couple of times going with Lou to Vera's Tall Girl's Shop for dresses to fit her five-foot eleven-inch frame. I helped Jackie pick out a dress or two I thought were really stunning. (Much, much later, after Memorial Day, 1955, she educated me with the female facts that, as many complements as she got from men on my dress picks, that she dressed to compete with women. Yet another real eye-opener into the facts of the male/female differences).

Jackie and I did, on occasion, fall asleep on the floor in front of the burning fireplace when Klaus brought Janice home. One night they discovered us asleep, cuddling on the floor in front of the fire. Had I kissed her yet? God, I have no memory of when I finally forced myself to hold her close enough to be able to kiss her. Oh, oh, thank God she cooperated far past my wildest dream. Our, my future became sealed with that first kiss. Utopia from then on. We were inseparable. Never felt really sorry for Doye.

NOVEMBER 24, 1954

It was Thanksgiving eve and the three Macs had been invited to ride, sitting on the back of a convertible, to parade down Hollywood Boulevard in the pre -Christmas parade. With the driver and me in front, driving west with all the beautiful Christmas decorations. One of the last times those beautiful, tall lighted-metal Christmas trees were used. The staging area was in a huge parking lot just east of the Pantages Theater at Hollywood and Vine.

While seated in the car, ready to go, right next to us – within five or six feet of our convertible, were Mohamad Ali, Joe Frazier, Sonny Liston and Archie Moore having great fun pushing and shoving each other around moment.

The 5.6-mile ride was another once-in-a-lifetime event for me.

The entire Christmas shopping experience with Lou and Jackie, plus the Day itself, are somewhere that I can't dig up from the ashes of love. All I can say, those days couldn't have been lovelier. Designed from above.

SUNDAY, JANUARY 2, 1955

When growing up as a kid I had always enjoyed going to Lake Arrowhead for summer camp recreation at our Junior High Schools Ag teacher, Mr. Wielding's room for twenty boys cabin. So much better than being farmed out to a "Y" camp every year. Big Bear Lake is another twenty-four miles further up the winding, two lane mountain top road. My mother considered it quite a common place rather than the luxurious Lake Arrowhead surroundings.

Since I had loved skiing for the past ten or so years, and there was snow all over the San Bernardino mountains at that time of the year and Big Bear was both cheaper and over a thousand feet higher elevation, Roger, Lou, Jackie and I, after the New Years' show on January second, decided to go for a few days and rent a cabin at Big Bear Lake until Thursday, because their Friday rehearsal day.

On that following day, Monday, very early, the four of us took off for Big Bear to the snow and possibly for them to learn some skiing. The bunny slope, hell, being basically a decent skier, in no way a hot shot, I had more damn fun getting Jackie to try and make it down that easiest slope. I have no idea what Roger and Lou were doing and could care less. I was where I wanted to be – with who I wanted, needed and had to be with.

I think it was on Wednesday night, late after dinner when Roger and Lou had gone to bed, we cuddled in front of the lovely burning fireplace, and kissing her was yet another great, glowing/growing time.

Getting ready to turn in, we decided to finish clearing the rest of the kitchen mess. As we tidied up the little mess left undone, why and how I got up the nerve is far beyond me, I blurted out, "Will you marry me?"

Without a moment's hesitation, she turned with, "Oh, YES! When?"

A very long and tender kiss followed. (Much later, just before the wedding, she confessed, 'I was ready to go to Las Vegas right then').

Early Thursday morning, knowing we had to pack and return down the hill, Lou and Jackie were finishing getting breakfast ready.

Giggling, Lou quips, "Well, I'm surprised you took so long."

After a quick sip from his coffee, Roger told Lou, "You know I win, Lou." Looking at me, "We've had a bet for …."

"Actually," Lou says, "The whole station crew was in on it. Leighton and …."

"… for months now," Roger finished with, as he started to leave to pack up and start for home.

SISTERS' CONFESSION

Why and how we decided to set Memorial Day, May 30ᵗʰ, for our wedding I have no memory of. But that was it. Monday after a Sunday show.

A month or so later, on our barely one-lane dirt path, just one hundred yards off Mulholland Drive, my tear-drop Studebaker sedan was parked overlooking the night lights of Hollywood far below and off to the Pacific and Catalina Island beyond. This was our favorite necking and talking or talking and necking spot. The hours we spent on that dirt road are what the greatest love stories are made of. They are slowly learning how to become one. The kissing and petting were just a very small part of those hours. Maybe not right then but, in retrospect where the concrete was poured for a forever love. It must have been after at least the thirty-first time there when Jackie pushed me slightly away.

Totally business like, "David, I have a real problem which I've just got to get rid of."

"Okay. Well, one thing I know for sure, you're not pregnant ... not by me, anyway. You haven't had time to ...."

She slugged me.

"Aw, shut up, damn you. Here I am, serious as hell with a great problem I want to unload and ...."

"Sounds very un-funny. My lips are sealed while my brain is scared to death of what you're about to dump on me."

She scowled at me with a stern look causing me, immediately, to become mute. Some silent moments while she fusses trying to find her best opening words.

Finally, "Okay ... Okay here goes." She pulled slightly away, to face me. "The MacDonald Sisters ... everyone thinks we're sisters."

I'm fast becoming stunned. "Is this what in hell this is all about?"

Fidgeting nervously, "Well ... well, we're not really sisters. We're ... well, two of us are sisters. The other girl is our double cousin. Do you know what a ...."

"I think ...."

"Well, two brothers marry two sisters. That makes them all with the same grandparents, aunts, relatives. Only not the same mother and father." Deep silent moments while all this confession sinks in. Both staring out the car window at the Hollywood night lights below.

Seemingly, many moments later, "Okay, David, if you had to guess or choose who would you want to be my real sister? Lou or Janice?"

More time in slow deep thought. "Oh, oh ... how I pray Lou."

"So sorry, dear, you lose."

"Oh shit. I just can't win, can I?" She grabbed me and drowned my disappointment with the best kiss she could produce while I tried to talk past her kisses.

Finally getting enough lip room, to say, "But ... I've spent almost every day with the three of you and when you mentioned Carrie and Arnold or ...."

"It'll take time to understand dear ... takes time." Searching her purse for something, "Carrie and Arnold ... well, as well as every other member of our family are the same for Lou, Janice and me. Only mothers and fathers are different for Lou."

Her questioning look back at me and, "Is it sinking in? Take your time. Take all the time you need. I can wait."

Taking a quick look out my driver's side window, "One hell of a shock after all these months and all the time the three of us have ...."

"At least Janice wasn't around us all those times."

"And all this time, since I've known all of you, the people in my family and those I work with have asked me, 'are they really sisters?'

I've always said, "I've have been with them for at least six to ten hours every day. They are sisters."

Silence while watching the city lights and off further into the full moon night.

TO DEARBORN,
FEBRUARY 22, 1955

Trying to remember the details of why Roger, Lou and Jackie moved from their Mansfield duplex, down on the flat, up onto Dearborn Drive in the Beachwood Canyon below The OLLYWOODLAND sign, I can't clearly recall. Lou and I think it must have been related to the fact that Mansfield went up for sale or Klaus wanted Janice to live alone. Also, Dearborn only had two bedrooms.

(Note: It took many years and a tremendous amount of frustration to reach the agreement to replace the H on that sign, which went down in the 1940's).

My Studebaker Cruiser was the best, quiet place for necking and wedding planning during the hours Roger and Lou were up. After that, in the living room. The car passion got extremely hot many times.

Working hard to get her to go all-the-way, she had to push me away with, "No, we've got to wait. Just cool down. It'll be great then. Only twelve weeks away. Let's work on the calendar now and cool down."

I had created an onion-skin calendar with thirty squares on it and ending on Memorial Day, May 30th. As an item on our list of wedding planning chores was accomplished, it was ticked off. Getting the wedding license. Blood tests. Deciding on the Grace Lutheran Church in Pasadena got the nod.

While growing up, I'd been involved with so many different religious churches my mother flitted through, that I had no religious preference. So, I easily went with Jackie's Lutheran choice.

We also found, and rented, a one-bedroom apartment in an area just below the Gates of Beachwood Canyon. Two of the apartments were completed, with the owner, a repossession muscle man for a finance company, trying to complete his third unit. The one next to ours was occupied by a young couple with a new baby.

We went to Sears Hollywood and ordered a King sized bed to be delivered by the twenty-ninth of May.

Since we were paying for the wedding event ourselves, it was not a lavish Hollywood ceremony. A small reception luncheon and photographer plus the cost of the church were all we could comfortably afford. Jackie's lovely dress was the costliest single item.

THE WEDDING, MONDAY MAY 30, 1955

The ceremony got underway with Dick singing an outstanding version of The Lord's Prayer.

Waiting on the riser, with the Reverend Victor Quello were, since my brother, Roger, was off in Saudi Arabia so he could pay Uncle Sam back for his abuse of the G.I. Bill, my buddy, Sid Cowles was my best man. Then my brother-in-law, Dr. Alan Trorey and another long-time friend, Don Wolf were holding me up.

At long last, I think it was close to noon, the organ starts the procession march. Led by Janice, followed by Lou, then Jackie's Matron of Honor, her mother, Beatta. Roger led Jackie down the aisle.

The ceremony itself was of wonderful length. Right to the point of making this most happy event legal. The exchanges of vows and then rings. The final Quello words of pronouncement and a quick kiss to seal the commitment forever.

Our Wedding

In the hall, after the dash back up the aisle, a kiss. Much, much more embarrassing, if done, on the riser, before the church audience.

The reception line ritual took quite a while. My mother joined us in greeting those attending. Bob and Dick, for sure. A few of Jackie's/Beatta's friends from Nebraska now living in Southern California, Klaus, along with all the top brass from KTLA, my NBC buddies as well as two of my dearest high school loves … with spouses.

The cake-cutting ceremony, complete with Jackie shoving her cut into my mouth, followed the buffet luncheon. Jimmie Haskell played his accordion for background music. What a great friend.

The final act of this play, out on the church steps, was Jackie throwing her flowers to the ladies grouped below. Then, the two of us, civilian dressed, jumped into our Study (she just had become co-owner), and making off, east, on Colorado Boulevard, back toward our spot in heaven, Big Bear.

Since our Study had only a bench seat, there's no space left between the two of us as I steer with only one hand. "Wow! It was over. As Jimmy Rogers sang in the song Jimmie did for him, *It's Over*.

Now to Big Bear for three days at Lakeside Logonita Lodge, before heading back down the hill to the Friday's next show meeting."

After the hour and forty-minute drive from Pasadena, forty-five minutes closer than from Hollywood, we arrived at the one-story Loganita Lodge on the south shore of the lake about 17:30, just in time for a quiet and peaceful dinner. A lovely stroll along the sand on the beach until dark enough to legally return to our room to prepare for that long-awaited promise: "It'll be great!"

Well…, it wasn't great. The strenuous day had taken its toll on my depleted energy.

Her soothing, boosting words of support failed. "Just relax. Too much excitement and…."

"Waited too long. Told you we shoulda practiced long ago. Weeks ago. We shoulda."

Quietly cooing, "It will happen, dear. Believe me, IT WILL HAPPEN. I guarantee."

Soooo, Tuesday and Wednesday were, during daylight, spent re-visiting the places we had hit our last memorable visit. The nights were a continuation of my inability to consummate this marriage. Her calming patience was hard to fight.

Another, almost as bad disappointment, returning to our new apartment for the first time as married people, we find that Sears did not deliver our new, king sized bed as promised several weeks ago. So, we were forced to ask my mother for the use of my old bed on Hoover. As fate would have it, Jackie's often promised reward did come to pass there, in my old bed. Not in our honeymoon bed in Logonita Lodge, but in my tired old bed on South Hoover Street.

The wild, out-of-the-blue gag I used when I was meeting the rest of the McDonnell family in Newman Grove in September, after the wedding, "well dear, let's go home and make a baby" turned out to be no joke at all. We had no hint that Jackie was already pregnant.

SUNDAY, JUNE 5TH

Back at KTLA – just recently moved from the old Melrose Theater to the new, large film production space, just off and behind the 52 Lane Bowling Lanes on Sunset at Van Ness. The Sunday rehearsal for Bandstand was underway. Roger worked with Leighton on stage. I was sitting in the second row, when the stage manager, Loring came from the control booth and to the front of the stage and down to where I sat.

"David, Klaus said that husbands aren't allowed at rehearsal ... would you please leave?"

Hearing this, Roger and Leighton exchange looks and looked toward the booth. This stopped most activity while they all waited for my reaction. I slowly looked around at every pre-show guest, such as art director Sherman's lady. I'd been at rehearsal ever since helping Roger copy the show...some seven or eight months now. I rose, shrugged and exited.

Out in the yard area stood the trailer-wardroom of the Macs. I knocked on the door and entered. The girls were rehearsing.

When they finished, to Jackie, "Honey, Klaus said that I can't be at rehearsal, and I have to leave."

A stunned exchange of looks between girls.

Lou opened with, "You've just gotta be kidding. I can't ... you've always been ...." A silent moment letting this sink in.

Slowly fuming, Jackie picked up her purse and grabbed my arm and pulled me toward the door. "See you later, ladies. Have a great show."

Janice and Lou were in a stupefied trance. I checked my watch as we left. Six hours 'til show time.

As we pulled out past the guard shack onto Van Ness, I pictured a huge fan about to be hit with the biggest load of turds you can imagine at the rehearsal. Aloud, "They're going to be blocking your number ...."

Sitting next to the passenger door and killing my subject matter, speaking straight ahead, she coolly says, "What about dinner at the Malibu Inn? I'll be able to eat something by then."

All I can offer is a silent nod of compliance and drive. Catching a quick peek several times to see how fuming she is. Never, never saw this side of her ever again.

Since the I-10 freeway was two years away, I had to wend our way on crowded surface streets.

After making it just past the Santa Monica pier, she checked the dash clock against her wristwatch.

"Okay. Let's go back. The girls need me."

We pulled into the studio truck entrance on Bronson, on the back side of KTLA. The sun has just set so it's not dark yet. She now slid across the seat to kiss me.

"Go park and sit with the audience. He can't stop you from doing that. I'll see you later." She got out of the car and disappeared past a scoring stage.

The show was flawless. Anything even close to that happening never happened again.

When driving to our home up Beachwood, two streets below the Gates, we turned left, up the hundred-yard-long Glen Holly Drive to the cul-de-sac where our apartment was, on the left. Since our place was up many steps, from our front window we could just barely see the OLLYWOODLAND sign

The Gates defined where we lesser names of The Canyon lived. People like Spring Byington, Aldous Huxley, Dimitri Tiomkin and so many names we'd see at the soda fountain in the drug store or in the

Beachwood Market lived above those Gates. One more I do remember, Stan Kenton, up on Holly Ridge Drive.

The drugstore's where I also met the great composer/arranger Johnny Mandel and started working with him from that time on.

Looking up the short steep paving, leaving the end of the cul-de-sac, was a small wooden one-story duplex about fifty feet up the slope. Sometime just after our wedding ... I have no memory of any of this part, Roger and Lou split. Never had a clue.

They got what I think must have been a silent one-day divorce. This is where Lou was happily living. Her neighbors are two great young men. Five foot six Rudy was a very well-known singer in Mexico City who has come to Hollywood to see if he could do better.

When? How soon after Lou moved in, and my brother, Roger had returned to the States on Labor Day, 1955, Lou became involved with her second Roger in a row. (That one lasted over sixty-five years).

Shortly after the Lower Mansfield Duplex broke up and Janice had moved into a solo apartment below The Gates on Beachwood, then Roger, Lou and Jackie moved into a two bedroom on Dearborn Drive in the hills which overlooked Beachwood Drive below.

Janice's apartment required that she farm her son four-year-old Johnny David out to a McDonnell cousin, Gertie, living out in the Duarte area at Klaus' insistence. This upset Jackie quite a bit, so we had to drive out to where Gertie was living to visit him. She was so extremely overwhelmed by that experience so; on the drive home I brought up the possibility of our adopting him?

That option was dashed within two weeks when we learned that our daughter Robin was on the way. No choice with that then.

MEETING
DR. PAUL REICHLIE

Just across from the Hollywood Men's Club, on Sunset Boulevard, were the medical offices of the doctor of my youth, Dr. Buell Sprague and his associates. Also, one to become a major player in our lives, Dr. Paul Reichlie.

Jackie came to feel she wanted her own doctor, so we went into the Sprague Building where I introduced her to head of the whole operation, red headed, seventy-plus, Grace.

Without a thought, Grace said, "We have the greatest OB-GYN on the west coast right in that front office down that short hall. Let me see if he's …." as she heads down that short hall, raps lightly and enters. Coming a short way back into the hall she waves and, "Great luck. He's had a cancellation and has at least a half-hour before his next lady."

As we pass her, "Boy, are you guys lucky."

"Thanks, Grace."

Jackie added "Oh yes, thanks so much. We seem to be very lucky." She introduced us to about sixty-year-old, six-foot, very nice and cheery looking, Dr. Paul Reichlie, shaking hands all around. He started with Jackie.

Smiling and holding her hand, "So nice meeting you ... well, both of you. My wife and I love Bandstand Revue and hate it if we miss it. A real pleasure." Still holding her hand, he turned to me and asked, "Why are you here? Are you involved with this?" With a laugh, he switched from her hand to mine with a quick shake and then back to Jackie's.

As Grace left, he gestured for us to take seats and went behind his desk to sit in his high-back chair.

"Now, let's get down to my business before my next lady arrives. She's usually late, but today she'll probably come on time. Just my luck." Addressing Jackie with, "It's you I want to hear from. He's just a bystander in this office. How might I be of service to you?"

"Well, I haven't had a checkup in quite a few years and think I, we need to find out what might be going on. My periods have been very irregular recently."

Leaning a bit forward, "Shall we make an examination" pointing at me, "while he goes out and annoys poor, nasty Grace some more ... if that's at all possible. About fifteen minutes should do it."

As he rose, we rose and they entered his examination room. I left for the outer area.

After some twenty-five or more minutes, Jackie came out into the waiting room to get me. "We're done. Come on back in."

I followed close behind her and we both took our same seats with Paul just settling behind his desk.

"Well," closing his file, "congratulations." To Jackie, "You are pregnant, my dear young lady. I'm so happy for you." To me, "I congratulate you also, Dad."

Great smiles and handshakes for all.

"Now, I must tell you my story ... assuming you want me to take care of you through all this?"

Still recovering from the surprise, we both were slow to react to his question. "Oh, sure." "Yes." "For sure."

"I must tell you the story of my operation here. I'm Catholic... but DO NOT practice in a Catholic hospital. I use Hollywood Presbyterian over on ...."

Coming quickly alive, I jumped in with, "I had my appendix out there in 1946 ...." pointing toward the outer offices, "by dear Doctor Sprague, out there."

"Good. Then you know your way there in a panic. More importantly, I don't go along with the Church thinking about, if forced to make a choice of which to save, the mother or the baby, I'd save the mother. The mother can usually, most always, have another baby. But a baby without its mother, I can't buy." He leaned back with, "Just as important—to me—is that I like to have a few drinks." Now directing his thoughts directly to her, "If I've been drinking, I'll be there to hold your hand and watch as my crew does the delivery. I want no mistakes blamed on my enjoying my few drinks."

She turned to me with a shaking-her-head smile, "And when I told you, long ago that I wanted to wait five years before having a baby, you agreed. You gave me your word. Okay, liar, David Perry Artemas Ward. You're in trouble, very deep trouble. It may take many years to get out of it."

After a lovely, appeasing dinner at one our favorite hangouts, Du Pars, and a quick visit to shock dear Lou, in her pad with the startling pregnancy news, we finally walked down fifty yards to and up our thirty-nine steps into our home. After that, some soothing Haagen Dasz coffee ice cream, and into bed.

WE BUY VERBENA DRIVE

The two as yet occupied apartments were built with the bedrooms up a short flight of stairs, with only one wall separating the two bedrooms. Slight noises could be easily heard from either side. The young couple across the wall's six month old baby could be quite noisy at times. That night, as we were cuddled in our bed, and her screaming started, it brought me to an immediate decision. "Jackie, we've gotta move. Buy our own house and move. Two screaming babies I can't take."

She turned on the bed light and sat up. "We can't buy a house. Move maybe, buy, we can't buy. We'd be thrown out within six months … if that long."

I reached over and turned the light off. "I'm gonna start looking tomorrow."

"You're nuts. Sleep it off."

"Two screaming babies I can't take."

After several days of checking the local bulletin board just outside the Beachwood Market, just inside The Gates, a canyon listing of a house a few blocks below The Gates on Verbena Drive showed up. Verbena ended up being a bit less than one hundred yards off of Beachwood. Up Verbena about forty yards, the snaky road turned an almost ninety degree right. On the left side of that ninety was the lovely sixteen hundred square foot two story home, with a sixteen-foot living room ceiling. Wide curving stairs up six feet to a wide landing with its two bedrooms off that landing.

The single lady owner showed us the house. We couldn't believe it, but the owner wanted to carry the paper. So, no need to clear credit with loan sharks or my bank. $15,000 total with $150 per month payments. A real steal, I couldn't believe. I didn't want to tap out our very small bank account, so I was able to borrow some bucks from my brother, Roger, for the small down payment. He was loaded after serving those eighteen very uncreative months in Saudi Arabia. And ... and he was now dating Lou. Seems Lou's attracted to Rogers?

So, we gave our notice to the apartment's bounty hunter owner and started collecting additional supplies for our new home, a few blocks away on Verbena Drive. Jackie slowly grew to lose her fear of losing our home by repossession.

BABY NAMING

My very pregnant Jackie sat on a stool out on our front porch, while I'm cutting her hair as we pour over possible baby name lists. Our baby naming deadline is just a few weeks away now ... in June?

(To explain why and how I became her barber, some months ago I'd driven her to a recommended barber way out on Sunset Boulevard, just two blocks before entering Beverly Hills. Her hair was naturally quite wavy and, at age twenty-one, was developing lovely gray streaks... which she hated. She also hated what the barber did. That was the last barber shop she went to. She trained me to both trim and do her color from then on).

We were at our first major wall of disagreement. She was unapproachable on this problem ... my problem, it seemed. "Well, if we can't have anything close to Jacqueline, then I'd like to...."

"You might think that I should say I'm sorry, but I won't. No way do I want my daughter—if it is a girl—to suffer being called 'Jackie Crackey' all through school. In Newman Grove, same kids at every level through high school in a town of twelve hundred." A quiet, stern moment and, "Well, as I've been saying, if it's a boy he'll have to be named David. That I...."

Changing from one side of her waves to another area, "Okay, I give in... part way, that is. No juniors though. No calling out 'David' and confusing both of us." "A little more right here," as she picked up a small hank of hair. "Just a bit ... Hey, wait a ... what about Robin?"

"For a boy? I don...."

"No, ya dummy. For a girl. A lovely songbird."

As I moved back around to the other side of her head, "What about ...," I turned back to face her, "... okay. Robin's great. But ... but I still want ... you"re holding out for David, so I'm holding out for something that I can get my way ... well, part way, anyway. Something starting with a 'J' like ... like ... like maybe Jan?" I stopped cutting and looked off, then back to cutting. "Hell no. Jon. Not J O H N, like a guy, but J O N. Male or female ... neutral?"

She broke out laughing, "Wonder if she'd get the boys' gym?"

Our usual dinner time being around 18:00, we had just finished off an angel-hair pasta with Hormel bean-less chili and homemade, heavily garliced, French bread toast.

After her last forkful, "Okay, okay, okay ... Jon Robin Ward works. We agree ... at last. Now, back to the David problem."

"Been working heavily on that one. When I was taking out the trash for the pickup tomorrow, in a paper I saw, I found something I really, really truly liked. Went back over it again and again. Tried to find any negative wh ...."

"Okay, Genius, please let me in on this great ...."

"Very simply put, Kirk?"

Complete stop and silence. She put her fork down, staring into the thought. Looked at me for a second. Back into more consideration.

"How ...?"

"The name Kirk means church, in Ireland." While sinking in and, "Then there's Kirk Klopp and Kirk Douglas. One, our creative genius dentist and the other a great movie hero."

Total silence for some time while this idea sinks further in. She picked up her plate and put it in the sink, braced against the counter, then turned to me.

"That's it. Ya nailed it."

While I let the second name grow on her, a bolt from the blue and, wow!

One more thought before ....”

“What else can we ....”

“I was given two middle family names and ... what if we ?”

With a harrumph, “Give a poor boy two middle names like ...?”

With that I got up and put my plate and glass in the sink after rinsing them off. With a shrug, “Hell. Just a thought.” I then moved to the door arch leading into the dining room and leaned against the jamb to mull the question over some more. As she continued straightening the out-of-place items in the kitchen, she became aware that I was still working on the boy’s naming situation. She shut off the spigot and looked at me. “What?”

Very slowly, “WELL, my brilliant Grandfather Louis and ... hmmm. That might work.” I moved to set the table for breakfast from the cupboards and drawers. “Then there was a very old family name connection I’d been told about, but am not sure....”

She sat on a stool while I set the table up around her. “Who might be able to know? Help solve your problem?”

“Admiral Oliver Hazzard Perry. Somehow, he won some great sea battle in the ... been told we’re somehow related.”

Adjusting my displacements, she admonished me with, “Forget all that. We’ve got David. That’s my must. We’ll call him Kirk, so you won’t get confused and for another ....”

Arriving at my final decision, “Louis. Just gotta be Louis. A great, calm mind. I’d never known one any better. David Kirk Louis Ward.” She takes two empty glasses from the table, handed me one and we clink and toast. In unison, “So be it! David Kirk Louis Ward.”

Once again, reflecting back on my office at Cameo Music, and how I got to know several of the people I worked for most of my young career there. One I’d met was composer Hoyt Curtin. He was doing mostly commercials and industrial films at that time. After some months of working at Cameo with him, I moved my office home and Hoyt followed my services there, so he got to know Jackie quite well. In later years, he became very involved with her voice on commercials and, as the head of the music Department at Hanna-Barbera, used her voice for many of their characters, like the singing voice for Cindy Bear. His work along with Jimmie's saw us through our pregnancy with Robin.

A very funny incident happened while we were scoring one of Hoyt's industrial films at Glen Glenn scoring stage with a large orchestra, while in our ninth month.

About two hours into the session, over the talk-back came, "Dave, phone home, it's your wife."

I moved quickly into the booth while Hoyt started another take. I came back on-stage as the orchestra finished. Several of the musicians were from Leighton's Bandstand group and were aware that we were very pregnant.

Turning to me, Hoyt asked, "Well …?"

Almost ashamed to answer, I finally had to say, "She just wanted to know when I'd be home for dinner."

A roaring reaction from the guys.

Jackie's mother, Beatta, had come west almost a month before to help us get ready for what was pending.

JUNE 4TH, 1956, WALKING ROBIN HOME

It was Sunday and Beatta had suggested that taking walks might wake the fetus into action. So, the three of us went to Griffith Park where Beatta and I played some tennis while Jackie walked around the court area in the very warm sun. Nothing came from that effort.

The next day, obviously a Monday, was our regular late-in-the-day visit to Paul's office.

We were in his examining room as he washed his hands, took a paper towel and addressed me. "Well, young man, many months ago you told me that you knew where Hollywood Pres was ... right?" I nodded yes. "Well, please take this wonderful, talented mother-to-be-shortly there, right now. No going anywhere but there. No home, no drive-in movie ... Hollywood Pres Hospital right now. Two miles east on Sunset, to Vermont. I'll meet you both there as soon as I can. They'll be waiting for you."

To Jackie, showing crossed fingers, "You're plus one right now, dear. I pray you don't have it in your car."

Quickly processed into Hollywood Pres, and being separated while she's made ready, I finally am called from the father's waiting area to join her about seven-thirty? She's propped up in bed and I'm holding her hand.

"They had to break my water. Things should move ...." labor pain... "Whew! That was a whopper. And to think I wanted to wait at least five years for this."

I'm now back, with and two other men and their relatives, in the waiting room about twelve-fifteen? While there, I did a lot of reflecting on a lot of our history and trying to make plans for what the future might dump on us.

Since we'd paid Paul's fee off a little each month and Jackie's AFTRA medical insurance paid the hospital off, we were mortgage free at that point.

At about one-fifteen, on the intercom, from Paul, "David, come on up and meet your lovely daughter."

As I leapt up, my thoughts, Jon Robin Ward...at last it's over...or really, just beginning.

At the delivery door, it opened with a nurse coming thru carrying a bundle and up to me, she opened the covers and introduced me. "Mister Ward, please say hello to your daughter."

"Hello, Jon Robin Ward."

I followed the two of them back into the room where Jackie was recovering. The nurse put our girl next to her and I leaned over and kissed them both.

I think we were really lucky since I now worked at home only. Cameo finished a few months ago. Gave up my copying desk to ex-Cameo slave, George Tipton.

Since Jackie had real trouble trying to nurse, we quickly evolved into the bottle feedings. Real teamwork here: I devised a system where Jackie does the ten o'clock feeding, kissed me good night, climbed the stairs and went to bed. I was working on Hoyt's film, *Thrillerama* at that time. I'd work and then do the two o'clock bottle thing. Then she'd get up and do the six o'clock feeding. That way, we both got plenty of sleep.

After about a month, thinking it would save trips up the stairs to check on Robin, I rigged a microphone over her crib. Great mistake.

Robin would roll over, causing an amplified sound and either Jackie or Beatta would race to check her out. Maybe every fifteen minutes or so?

After about a week of that stress, my brilliant system was scrapped, and Robin did very well without being needlessly disturbed.

In early 1956, Klaus, was medically proclaimed cancer free. So, his wedding to Jackie's true sister, Janice, was a major Hollywood event on Valentine's Day, 2/14/1956 in Klaus' home, on the hill overlooking Hollywood, below. The guest list was made up of the most important names at KTLA, crew and stars as well as from the television industry.

MEETING DR. SOFI

I can't remember the exact social event, but the time was a Saturday night in April of 1956 when Jackie and I had just left a social event which required that we were dressed up. When we reached our Woody Wagon, she came up with, "Gee, such a great time. We're dressed up for the first time in a long time and nothing to do ... no place to go."

Reaching for the car door handle, I came up with, "Heck, ya got any ideas? What'd you like to...."

She took my arm to stop me from opening the door. "Hey ... hey, what about calling Bertha and seeing ...."

Such an out-of-left-field idea really stopped me with, "Gee. Don't know if...." Settling into the passenger seat, "let's find a phone.

Come on, she can only say no ... if they're home, that is."

With a giggle at her thought, "They couldn't say no if they aren't home, can they? Well, can they?"

Bertha Sanders was a woman in her late 60s who was a dear friend of my mother's. She was a psychic who had tremendous history in Hollywood. Until the war years of the forties she had an office building on Highland Avenue, across from Hollywood High School. Among her clients were the three Barrymores, Valentino, Harlow, and Gable. But she was forced to close her office because Los Angeles County outlawed commercial psychics.

My mother was a noted numerologist who had reasons to deal with friends like Bertha; to trade their gifts. In my late teens, on occasions, I would go with mother to visit Bertha. And here are a couple of her stories I was connected to. One was that my sister, Ginny, would marry a man for her second marriage, who had the same name as one of my mother's sons. Ginny married Doctor Jake Perry. One of my middle names being Perry.

For me, in my early 20s, she said that I would marry a woman who she could only describe it was that I was a dress designer and that my wife would wear the clothes I designed. OK, so I wrote the music. And she sang it.

Bertha, with her husband, Terry, lived on. Lexington Ave, in Hollywood, which is just above Santa Monica Blvd. and east of Van Ness Ave.

My mother invited Bertha and Terry to our wedding where she met and became connected with Jackie. We had an open invitation to visit anytime. After Robin was born, she would come to our Verbena Drive house and hold séances for some close friends.

Luckily, we found a parking spot in front of the house next door and had just reached the front door when Bertha opened it and ushered us in with, "What a pleasant surprise. Here our small party has just broken up and you lovely young people arrive to brighten us old folks up."

There are three other couples just leaving the long table and are introduced to us. These people are all psychics who, every so often, get together to delouse their psychic selves, which they can't do to themselves.

Almost immediately a tall, mid-seventies man, Dr. Sofi, approached us, took Jackie's hand and blurted out, "Your sister is pregnant, and she doesn't know it. She will have a boy. The father will die and never see his son."

After a few more words from him, then Bertha moved Jackie off to deal with some of the others. Coffee and desserts were passed out while Dr. Sofi took me aside and explained how he'd become psychic.

"My wife is Icelandic, and they are quite often very psychic. I always thought she was a little nuts...but I loved her anyway."

He sipped some coffee and continued with his captive audience. "As an engineering scientist, working for the government, I finally set up a trap to make her see how wrong she's been for all those years. I told her I wanted to take her on a surprise vacation. That's all I told her. Just it would be a surprise. From D.C, we drove straight through to Chesterfield, Indiana to their annual Psychic Fair.

When we got there, she was pleased but mad at me thinking I was up to no good. After that week there and those experiences I—we both— had, I went home a totally changed man. Being truly psychic can be a huge curse." Looking strangely at me, "you're quite a psychic yourself. Don't let it rule your life."

The next morning being Sunday show day, just after lunch, in their dressing trailer, the three Macs were getting ready to rehearse. Jackie stood back eyeing Janice up and down with her arms folded. She smoothly, with an authoritative sounding voice, said, "Janice, you're pregnant."

Janice was shocked and Lou broke out in a roar.

Completely flustered, Janice stumbled out, "Wha ... wha ... no way. What are you... what are you saying? Pregnant? Not a chance, little sister."

Things quieted down and the girls continued getting ready for the show.

Well, three weeks later Janice learned that she was truly, in fact, pregnant. At age 40, Klaus would die during her sixth month as Dr. Sofi had predicted.

A huge surprise to Jackie and me, of how extremely quietly Lou and her first Roger had separated and she was suddenly living in a split-shared cabin 50 yards from us up the dead end of our Glen Holly. Details never disclosed about the separation or divorce.

MY BROTHER ROGER
MEETS LOU

My little brother (thirteen months younger and only6'2.5"), Roger, returned from an eighteen-month tour of duty in Saudi Arabia on Labor Day. His chore in going to Saudi was to pay off Uncle Sam for the GI Bill he'd wasted which is why he couldn't be my best man at our wedding.

He had abused his Uncle Sam by taking the G.I. Bill money and then going to the Santa Monica beach almost every day, with his buddy Dick Haltom, and a case of beer, rather than attend any UCLA classes ... for two semesters.

Now buying himself off his Uncle's Shit List, he bought a new Pontiac coupe and several long, long dreamed of hunting rifles ... with reloading equipment set up in his home at 120 South Hoover.

Very soon thereafter, he showed up at the KTLA Studio to visit Jackie and me and take in the routine of getting our show on the air at eight o'clock every Sunday night. That's the day when The Fan met its future energy source...he met Alyce Lou. (Lou standing 5'10 and Rog 6' 2.5") hit it off immediately ... sixty-five years' worth.

From after-show sessions on Sunday night until the following Friday show meetings, we had a lot of fun time together, the four of us. Bowling, dancing, miniature golf, along with surfing at the beach in Malibu.

Another fun—kinda fun fact: Lou didn't have to learn another man's name. She could just continue calling out 'Roger' and not make a mistake.

In early 1956 Klaus, was medically proclaimed cancer free. So, his wedding to Jackie's true sister Janice was a major Hollywood event. On Valentine's Day, 2/14/1956 in Klaus' home, on the hill overlooking Hollywood, below, the guest list, was made up of the most important names at KTLA, crew, and stars as well as from the Hollywood television industry.

There was a Los Angeles Times front page headline:

𝕶𝖑𝖆𝖚𝖘 𝕷𝖆𝖓𝖉𝖘𝖇𝖊𝖗𝖌 𝕮𝖗𝖊𝖆𝖙𝖔𝖗 of 𝕶𝕿𝕷𝕬 𝕯𝖎𝖊𝖘

Klaus died on September 16th, 1956. He was just two months into his fortieth year. His newlywed wife, Janice, was in her sixth month of her pregnancy when he left us.

The funeral ceremony was overflowing. A tremendous group attended the Catholic funeral and burial service in Inglewood.

Quietly remembering Klaus' genius for taking the late 40's infant television introduction into its first giant leap into what the rest of the industry followed as fast as they could figure out how and were able.

If they said, "it couldn't be done," Klaus proved them wrong so many times. Following are just a few of the things he forced KTLA to accomplish:

KTLA covered the industry-considered TV impossible first atomic blast in the Nevada desert in January 1951 by putting signal relay dishes on the backs of crew members and having them carry them to the top of every peak between the KTLA transmitter on Mount Wilson for line of sight through the Sierra Nevada Mountain range to the blast scene way out in the Nevada desert.

They also covered out-of-area news events thought impossible: The Tragic three-year-old Kathy Fiscus death in San Marino after falling into a partially covered well in early April 1949. No other station had tried remotes of this magnitude until KTLA proved their worth. They were on the air for 27.5 continuous hours.

My buddies and I just happened to be sitting at the bar in The Blue Room, on La Brea and Third Street. We were so moved by what KTLA was broadcasting, that we drove the almost an hour out to that San Marino site to experience that tragedy firsthand.

Third, but in no way the least, it was said, TV cameras are too heavy to fly. Well Klaus, and two of his engineers John Silva and Roy White proved that a telecopter was possible and could get off the ground and really fly.

Those are just a few of KTLA's firsts under Klaus' creative role in the beginning of television.

It took the hostile New York home office less than two months to dismantle all of Klaus's expensive musical shows. He'd fought that New York Home Office for years with, "The musical greats we have make us one of the most watched outlets in our area, so other sponsors fight to get use of our airtime."

All of them: Spade Cooley, Orrin Tucker, Bandstand Revue, with the three McDonald Sisters, Ina Ray Hutton Orchestra, Western Varieties. Lawrence Welk and Klaus had gotten into the highest-level snit and Welk took his, now very successful show and left KTLA for ABC and continued the success created by Klaus and his KTLA. New York's hammer hit hard and heartless without Klaus fighting back. So, we were all very quickly unemployed.

Within days after Klaus was laid to rest, Janice was medically diagnosed as needing to stay off her feet. Don't recall/remember, but the legals of closing out Klaus's estate and home slowly forced Janice into some other care option.

Jackie and I, now both KTLA unemployed, came up with the idea that Janice might live on a hospital bed, on our balcony, just outside of Robin's room door. That marvelous Verbena Drive home we'd bought, which Jackie was convinced we'd be repossessed from within months, had a living room only described as one which a scenic director might create:

Off the approaching front deck our front door opened into a sixteen-foot ceiling scene in a 20x35 foot room. Then up a semi-circular staircase and across the back wall, a twenty-four-foot landing about six feet above the main floor. Two bedroom doors off the landing. The last door was Robin's, the first ours.

The height of the ceiling gave us the wonderful opportunity of having the tallest Christmas trees we could get through the door. Much like what we had in my Berkeley home, as a kid.

CAMEO MUSIC, 1950

Taking a big step backward to explain my entry into the business world of Hollywood music from my beginning in 1950, my tremendously lucky years at Cameo Music.

After Fox West Coast Theaters quietly let me go from my assistant manager's job at the famous Egyptian theater on Hollywood Boulevard for uncovering the money hanky-panky between the manager, his wife (other assistant manager) and his sister-in-law cashier, I was looking for a new line of work.

Since I had several years with the Fox West Coast Theaters chain, and on several occasions helped promote a new film opening, and my grandfather had been connected with Louis B. Mayer, I tried MGM to get work in their publicity department.

So, dressed in my best dark blue suit, I arranged an appointment with the lesser-known at that time Dore Schary. We met in Mayer's old office.

Schary said to me, "David, as far as the publicity department goes, I can get you hired in the mail room first—at least for a couple of years. Then you'll work your way up the very long ladder through various minor jobs until possibly, very possibly an opening in the publicity works happens. Guessing, maybe six or seven years.

The serious way he presented this routine I felt he was being totally honest. Then he added, "Tomorrow, I can put you in the acting class and you'll possibly develop into a much better pay scale in a matter of months."

After a very short thought session, I stood, thanked him and left that dream behind me.

My so-very-long Fairfax High buddy's sister, Peggy, was working for an employment agency somewhere, trying to get me a job, Peggy called and said, "Dave, I just happened to see on the card you filled in that you studied music at LACC. Right?"

Trying to grasp a connection to her question, "yep. No degree, just learning music structure for a year and a half. Two classes a semester. Really interesting. Harmony structure, chord progressions and the best were a class, first time taught in the west, Acoustical Physics. Makes me wish I'd learned the piano rather than fight my teachers ... and my mom, who was one hell of a pianist."

Peggy, quite coyly, "I have a six-week temp job for you in a music shop in Hollywood, while we find you a better, more secure job. Better than nothing for six weeks while I'm looking."

Getting all the pertinent info from her, I made my way to 1527 ½ Vine Street. One hundred yards north of Music City on the corner of Sunset and Vine streets, left, down small alley between the old ABC and Spotlight bar leading to the NBC overflow parking lot, a left to see the Cameo Music sign with wooden steps leading up the back of the building to a porch for entry into Cameo.

The wooden steps, each one carried part of these words, "Up These Steps Climb the Greatest Musicians and Composers in the World."

Across the outside balcony and down two steps into an overpowering smell of ammonia from two blue printing Ozalid machines. At the front desk sat Celia Buck, knitting. She rose to greet me and I introduced myself. She quickly called the real chief of operations over, Joe Valle, and she asked Joe to see if I could be of use for those temp weeks.

I passed the test so husband Ron and Celia could tour South America somewhere. Ron Buck was the owner who bought Cameo to give his wife something to do when their son went off to college. He had a music take-down service for songwriters in an office next to Nickodel's on Ivar, two and a half blocks from Cameo. Celia's brother, Bill Penzer, owned an entire square city block in Westwood.

Celia was extremely reluctant to hire me, but their trip would need to be cancelled if she didn't cave in ... reluctantly. "Only while we're gone."

When they returned, Joe quietly took her aside with, "Celia, we will never do better. This fellow is what we've needed for so long."

Over a period of a year and a half, Celia and I became great buddies. I conned her into getting a motor scooter to save my walking many blocks to publishers and song writer's offices to pick up and deliver parts. Saved one hell of a lot of time, and my legs.

Cameo had a space approximately12x12 for the Bob Ross Music Copy Service. Bob had three copyists in there full time, and, when panicked, had two more leaking out into the Cameo desks when in a panic. His crew did all the Cameo client's lead sheets they could manage.

During that period, Celia would give me a composer's new song to take home at night to try to hone my very poor penmanship I'd used for several of my mother's pupil's material. I was slow and required quite a bit of coffee into the wee hours. Almost all new songs were 32 bars long: Two same eight bar phases, one eight bar bridge and the first eight repeated to end the song. If four notes per bar it took eight music lines with title and credit space above for most songs to fit on the 9x12" vellum paper so the Ozailid machines could make as many copies the writer wanted at $.07 cents a copy.

Finally, about mid-1952, Copyist Bob had had it ... the space problem. He moved his growing mess into a building two blocks away. Plenty of desk and library storage space.

So, Celia offered me Bob's old desk and got Nelson Riddle's copyist, Ted Bergren to share the space.

I was so damned fortunate to deal with, service and meet and work with/for the most famous names of music and Hollywood beyond any dream in my sixty-eight-year career.

Jimmie Haskell, Johnny Mandel, Stu Phillips, George Tipton,

Dimitri Tiomkin, Miklos Roza, Leonard Bernstien, Bob, Dick and Al Sherman, Jay Livingston & Ray Evans, Jerry Livingston, Haven Gillespie, Brian Wilson's dad, Johnny Mercer, Don Raye & Gene DePaul, George Anthiel, Hank Mancini and many, many others.

Actors such as ultra-quiet and charming, Lew Ayres of the Dr. Kildare film series, great character actor, Will Wright, top star Preston Foster, who had an Irish musical act with his wife. The gal who had just driven across the country from New York with her then writing partner Lou Spence in a Volkswagen convertible coupe, Marilyn Keith ... to later marry Alan Bergman and together they won three Oscars.

Marilyn once handed me a sheet of music paper with a copy of her new song, in pencil. My confusion caused me to ask, "Okay, Marilyn, why this pencil copy of ...."

She cut me short with, "I'm showing this to Sinatra and I want him to think that he's the first to see this song."

One day in late 1952, Sheridan Pearlman entered our doors and Celia stood to service him. From my office I remembered Sheridan from Fairfax High and moved out to greet him with our famous Fairfax High chant: "Rat-a-tat-a-ching-ching hobble goggle razzle dazzle ding, Hong Kong chow, Fairfax High School, wow!"

He broke up. "Wow! It's sure been years since I've ...."

Taking his arm I turned to introduce him to Celia. "This fella was in every aud call show we had at Fairfax High ... squeezing his accordion. Sheridan ...."

With a slightly embarrassed grin, he interrupted me with, "I'm Jimmie Haskell now," he nodded and shook hands with her.

A slight pause and continued with the introduction, "Celia Buck here is the main whip here, but her husband, Ron signs the checks."

He turned to me, "You work here?"

Pointing, Celia piped up with, "David and Teddy run our music copying office in there."

An impressed look. "You're a copyist?"

She reached out and patted my arm, "One of the best."

Now beaming Jimmie, "Wow! What a coincidence. My boss, Mister

Lew Chudd, told me about you folks here at Cameo so I came up here looking for copying help. I've just started working with Imperial Records and they've given me a Ricky Nelson session to do next week."

As I lead him toward the copy office, he continued with, "Since I have the worst penmanship west of the Mississippi, just must work with a copyist. Are you available?"

BACK TO 1955

Soon after Jackie and I were married, at the end of May, 1955, another great time in my music history. Dennis Farnon came off the Cameo entrance balcony and stepped down the two steps into the overwhelming ammonia aroma.

Joe moved from the master worktable to meet him. "I was told you have a music copying service here and ...."

Joe pointed into the copy office, where I happened to be by myself, with, "In there are the copyists."

He then moved toward my office with, "thanks."

I put my note making pen in its holster and rose to meet him at the doorway. "Hi. I'm David Ward ... the only one here right now. Ted's across the street at NBC."

As we shake hands, "Hi. Nice to meet you. I'm Denny Farnon. I'm new here ... in L.A. from Chicago and was just asked to bail out a Mel Torme session at Capitol. Do you work on scores?"

With a slight grin, "Transposed or concert?"

A huge grin as he asked back at my question. "Do you run into concert scores much?"

Pointing toward Ted's empty chair we both sat. "Rarely, but the answer is, yes. On occasion. One client. A bit slower and more costly with all those horns transposing."

After about fifteen minutes exchanging our personal history stories, we went down Vine to Coffee Dan's for a snack. This is where I learned that the three musical Farnon brothers were Canadian. The two other well-known Farnons, Brian, the oldest, was the orchestra leader at the Chez Paree in Chicago until it was to close in 1960. Composer and arranger Robert was now in England and had become nicknamed the Henry Mancini of Europe.

Jimmie's Score

Shortly after my first session with Denny, he was hired as head of the RCA West Coast Albums Department which allowed him to schedule the orchestra when we were ready with the four arrangements per session. If it was a seven o'clock date, on occasion we'd have dinner with our friend the recording engineer, we were that casually prepared.

Independently he was able to work for producers like Jay Ward Productions creating the music for Rocky and His Friends, Bullwinkle and Fractured Flickers as well as the Mr. Magoo cartoon series. On one

Magoo he used my daughter, Robin's toy sewing machine to make the whirring sound when Magoo had to run on top of a huge printing press to escape falling back into the gears. Another of Robin's toys was a ten-note toy piano which the piano player would play for an effect on his *The Mother Magoo Suite* on which Marni Nixon, dubbed, 'The Ghostess With The Mostest' sang two songs.

Probably the last thing I'm going to write of the numerous wonderful stories I have of the wonderful times I/we had with him is the small part I was involved with as NARAS (the National Academy of Recording Arts and Sciences … the people who give out the Grammys) was created.

The founding members were Jesse Kaye, of MGM records, Lloyd Dunn and Richard Jones of Capitol records, Sonny Burke and Milt Babler of Decca records and Dennis Farnon of RCA records. Very shortly after that meeting, at the Brown Derby restaurant on Vine Street, in Hollywood, Axel Stordahl, Paul Weston and Doris Day of Columbia Records all joined in to help form NARAS and created the Grammy Awards.

The night after that original meeting, Denny was asked to re-create a re-hash of the twelve arrangements that Harry Belafonte had recorded in New York, *Belafonte Sings the Blues*. Harry was very dissatisfied with most of what he did there and those arrangements. Harry wanted all twelve songs ready for the first session so he could make his choice, on the spot, as to what he felt like singing. Of course, there were only four sides to be done on the three-hour session, but he wanted all twelve ready which required a rare 40-hour day working with Denny, for me.

I had to work at his home, on the kitchen table, on Bonnie Hill drive overlooking the then Monkey Farm Island in the middle of Cahuenga Pass, just off of Barham Blvd. This way I could do each arrangement as Denny finished them. It was great that there were only 10 players in the group, but all twelve arrangements were ready for the first session. While during this long, all afternoon, all-night, all-day session, Denny's wife, Christine, was typing/creating the documents preparing forms so

NARAS could be created. Chris was, at that time, executive secretary to Alan Livingston, head of Capitol records. The Farnons had a brand-new baby, so Chris was chored between taking care of the baby, typing, cooking for Denny and me and again typing far into the night.

Over the years, at least three times, while Denny was alive, I had petitioned NARAS to give him a Grammy rather than the marble cigarette box -shown here. They refused each time, saying, "It had to be earned." Now, of course, they give away complimentary Grammys as they see fit. Since Denny passed away in May of 2019, I still think it's interesting to pursue having a Grammy beside the cigarette box on his family's shelf.

The Cigarette Box

After we'd worked together for a while and I'd moved my work home, he'd write an arrangement and deliver it to our home around four-thirty or five each day and Jackie would ask him to stay for dinner. Finally, that almost daily routine became expected.

While wasting time for dinner, we'd play chess using my nicely modified 3x6'8 door for a coffee table set on four 16" concrete blocks for legs.

The memory just recalled, on several occasions, the great group singer, Tom Kenny, would join us in chess and easily beat both of us.

After dinner, an awful lot of fun, with him playing the piano for Jackie to sing while I worked on his latest arrangement. They were always working out vocal arrangements together. Interesting that he never used her on sessions where there were background singers. His groups usually required eight voices with a large orchestra. No small rock and roll groups like the Wrecking Crew.

Over time, she became Jimmie's vocal contractor whenever three girl backup singers were needed.

WE MEET B.J. BAKER

While Robin, our first, was still bassinet sized, my Cameo replacement, George Tipton introduced us to B.J. and Buddy Baker. B.J. was the mother of Mickey Rooney Jr and Timmy Rooney ... second wife of Mickey Rooney. Buddy was a major composer at Disney. B.J. was Miss Alabama of 1944 and a great singer, an alto in Jackie's range.

With Robin in our traveling bassinet, we'd drive to the Tarzana area of the Valley in our 1948 Pontiac woody wagon for a wonderful evening a couple of times a week. The girls had great fun making up clever duets from Buddy's suggestions.

They became great friends and Jackie got B.J. out of the house by doing bootleg commercials for a beginning.

Note: B.J. sang the voice of Nancy Kwan in The Flower Drum Song. She beat Jackie in joining the Anita Kerr Singers. I told her, "Don't worry. She'll screw up within a month or two and Anita'll be calling for help". I was right. It took just over two months. Twice more, B.J. screwed up cross-mixing sessions and many top vocal contractors gave up on her. Jackie was with the Kerr Group until Anita retired.

I had great fun teaching Jackie to read music. I talked her into going to LACC and getting top help with reading. Her great musical ear made it an easy, fast learning process.

While I was working on Jimmie's arrangements, I'd do the voice parts first so Jackie could practice reading her part. When Jimmie started using three girls, Jackie became his vocal contractor. She'd read the parts at home and was well up on each arrangement before she delivered the first three arrangements to the session while I fought the fourth done. After a bit more than a year she didn't want to rehearse anymore. She was well ready to read at sight.

DECEMBER 7, 1956

On that same date which will go down in American history—some years before however—Lou and her second Roger were married. Of course, at this Ward wedding I got to be Roger's Best Man. Our sister Ginny was Matron of Honor with her two daughters, Sharon and Kathy acting as flower girls. Our mutual great buddy, and my best man, Sid Cowles helped me get Roger through it all. Jackie sang solo because Janice was still bed-ridden.

Klaus Rory was then born January 5, 1957 and Klaus never saw him.

A few weeks after the Roger and Lou wedding panic calmed down, Lou was setting dinner in their apartment while Roger opened yet another beer.

Holding a plate above the place on the table it would end up, she asked, "Now that we're both unemployed, do you have some great ideas what ...?"

Shaking his head, he crossed to the small table to squeeze her, taking a sip, "Ya know Lou, having been a corpsman in the navy ... and always been fascinated with medicine, I've wondered, since starting my ... our new life, I'd like to try it ... become a doctor. That was my direction at UCLA where I screwed up so badly."

She patted his arm with, "Dear, if you didn't screw up with Dick and were forced to Saudi, we might have never met?"

Quiet moments, with fondling hugs and a kiss, she continued with, "It's a great ... now's the time, dear. The time to go all-out for it. Not stuck with jobs we have to give up. No reason to fight what we'd be giving up here and ...."

He released her, sipped and moved about the room looking at the window wall, "But, you know, that's why I had to go to Saudi with Bechtel. I missed David and Jackie's best man spot. I fucked up with Uncle Sam's GI Bill. Took Sam's money so Dick and I could spend all our days with a case of beer at Santa Monica beach rather than the UCLA medical classes."

She put two loaded plates on the table, and they sat. Quiet moments of deep thought.

She slowly put her fork down and with a fierce look, "okay ... damn it ... okay ... what if we move far away from Santa Monica beach, Dick and UCLA?"

Starring hard at her, finally, "So ... so, where is this going? Where, how ...?"

Defiantly, "Let's move to Omaha. You connect with the University people in Lincoln. As an ex-navy corpsman of the Korean War, at your age, I think, I'd hope they'd respect your application more than any eighteen- or nineteen-year-old kid, just out of high school."

The following several weeks of getting those plans worked out were quite emotional for the three Ex MacDonald Sisters as that show biz era ended for them.

Loading a U-Haul trailer attached to Roger's new Pontiac was a very simple, quick, process.

I was always curious why, with Lou's years as a featured character on Bandstand Revue, why she didn't approach the Omaha advertising community about doing commercials?

They drove east on I-5 until they moved onto the I-70 which took them all the way into Nebraska, and their new life of hope.

Since Lou was our favorite McDonnell sister, it was easy to have great fun helping Lou and Roger to easily fall into their relationship, which lasted so well those years from 1955 until October 2021

One of the great contacts we fell into by BJ and Jackie doing as few bootleg commercials was meeting Al Allen. Al was a hyper energetic enthusing young commercials agent working out of San Francisco who much preferred working with all of the available talent here in Hollywood. And he loved flying down south using one of his best client's airplane service, PSA or Pacific Southwest Airlines. "PSA Gives You a Lift" was the first commercial client Jackie sang for with Al.

Interesting aside: PSA was based in San Diego with only four aircraft. (Buy ad for $5.99)

A little more backstory: PSA started with only four planes which were scheduled from 05:00 until 24:00. From midnight until takeoff they were serviced at their home port, SAN.

Their routing, SAN to LAX to SFO to LAX and back to SAN. They finally added Portland (PDX) their longest airtime, one hour and fifty minutes.

The first time we were introduced to PSA was after eight singers—four guys and four gals—planned to fly on United to San Francisco to perform on an Ernie Ford TV show, but were held over for a second spot and we lost our return flight to LA. I went along so Jackie and I could ask my dad to the show and visit.

So, one of the guys who happened to be the transportationist for the four guys, re-booked us on PSA for home. When checking in, an agent ticked us off the list on his clipboard and handed each of ninety-eight passengers a numbered plaque about the size of a large donut ... and we waited.

Almost exactly on time their DC-7 came roaring off the runway, turned sideways and stopped ... leaving the motors idling. Two ramps, one forward and a second nearer the tail were pushed into their position and the doors both thrown open. Within not more than five minutes, the passengers had de-planed and with the doors still wide open, we could see the entire crew cleaning the plane interior. (Those PSA stewardesses were dressed ready for a Playboy cover. None over 24 years?)

That cleaning and straightening operation had to take less than five minutes.

With a waving signal from Miss America in the cabin, our agent threw open the door to the ramp we used and, as we passed him, we handed him our numbered doughnut and made our way onto the plane.

Doors were slammed closed, locked and the engines came to a roar as we moved into our takeoff position.

Not more than fifteen minutes from doors opening to closing. And the fare from SFO to LAX was $12 per seat. And PSA was AL's client.

One last Al story: Some higher up in Al's San Francisco Commercial agency had a young lady—maybe 21? —who wanted to sing commercials. So, south Al came with the young diva and her support girlfriend. We worked in Radio Recorder's small dubbing voice-over studio. It was booked for half an hour.

The charming, excited girl made mistakes on her own and had real trouble making her vocal animated enough in the phrases Al needed in the 20 second spot. She went just short of twenty-five minutes and then Al had Jackie take over. The first take was what Al wanted but, "let's take one more for protection."

I was at the coffee area in the hallway when the singing girls passed with her support saying, "So, you wanna sing commercials do ya?"

At home, while copying parts, I was able to babysit Robin while Jackie was at her music classes at LACC. Who was our house help then? Margie? Not Ruth until Keith and new addition.

THE GUY MITCHELL
TV SHOW,
OCTOBER 1957

In late October of 1957, Janice and Jackie got to work on the Guy Mitchell TV show with three boy singers. That wonderful gentleman, legendary music master Van Alexander was the orchestra leader while my friend, Clint Romer, was the show's copyist, so it was very easy for me to also work that show.

That gig only lasted one TV cycle ... thirteen weeks, starting in October and ending just after Christmas in January of 1958

Holy shit! Somehow, I have no idea how ... where ... when ... only kidding. I did know how Jackie had become pregnant again, though it was not expected nor planned. A true Karmic Must?

Since our expected due date was forecast as early April and the show's thirteen-week cycle was not picked up, the AFTRA insurance coverage ran out for us on January first.

We were at home, near the end of January, readying for the number two birth. Okay, our income was now down to one ... mine. Jackie couldn't work ... except for Jimmie and occasionally with B.J.

We'd made monthly payments to Paul to insure his cooperation at the critical moment. We'd faithfully visited Paul every two weeks until March when the visits were deemed to be necessary once a week.

Luckily my work with Jimmie and Hoyt kept us from falling into debt.

APRIL 1, 1958

That trip to Hollywood Pres was much easier this time. No urgent 'almost too late' rush. We'd had a running joke about not having an April Fool's Day delivery.

About 01:30 on April 2nd, 1958, with two other eagerly expecting fathers in the waiting room, a masked nurse enters and asked, "Mister Ward?"

I moved quickly toward her.

"Mister Ward, please come and greet your new son."

A slight applause from the other two fathers there as I followed the nurse through the open door and down two doors to the one, she held open for me to enter.

Jackie was in bed holding a quite pink newborn partially covered body in her left arm. I crossed and gave her a kiss and added, "what a great moment. How did it go? How ...?"

"Not fun, but a bit more used to how it goes after Robin." A slight giggle and "Ow!" Looking down, she commanded, "I've told you; his name is David ... David Kirk Louis Ward ... and that's it. Nothing else. David Kirk Louis ... we'll just call him Kirk as you thought up. Liked your thinking on that one. But I won't have two David's in my house at the same time."

She then handed me David Kirk Louis to carefully hold and admire.

I was so enjoying this first moment in our new history with a slight shake of my head, and handed Kirk back to his mother, where he belonged. As we've discussed quite a bit lately, one major dilemma right now. Paul's paid off. Thank God, but the AFTRA insurance won't cover the hospital costs. That help all stopped when we lost the Guy Mitchell Show just a month too early. Figure he'll cost like Robin, about two hundred, plus a bit?

Leaving her smiling at Kirk, seriously, I continued thinking what if ... how ...? With a deep sigh, "Since Roger's out of our loan range, gotta get .. .maybe borrow from Jimmie ... or Hoyt or wherever. Got just two days to bail you two outta here."

Having just arrived home and opened the front door, the phone began ringing. I left my keys dangling in the partially opened door, as I rushed to answer.

"Oh, hi Jim. Need your congratulations. Jackie just delivered us a son." After listening a moment, "David Kirk Louis. Jackie threatened a divorce if other than David. But we're calling him Kirk so there won't be two Davids in this house."

A moment listening and, "chose Kirk since a Kirk is an Irish church and Kirk Klopp, our dentist is such a strong and successful guy ... and then there's Kirk Douglas, another very strong character."

I was now seated at my desk, next to our upright piano.

"Aw, come on, Jim. Are you kiddin' me?" A pause to listen. "Wait a minute, please. Please wait a sec. Gotta catch my breath. Are you ...?" Another pause. "Ozzie said he's going to put Rick's album on the show and ...." The excitement in my voice was growing more each second. I slowly rose and moved toward the sofa next to my desk. "He wants my re-use bill for two hundred and forty to ...." I'd now flopped onto the sofa and was ecstatic. Using very slow words, "Jim ... wow! Ozzie and Rick just bailed my new son, David Kirk Louis, out of Hollywood Presbyterian in two days."

During the next few months, Robin, just a few weeks shy of two years old, had great fun helping Mom with holding Kirk's bottle and a few other fun things for both girls.

Another great twelve-foot Christmas tree in the living room corner which Rob had fun keeping our now crawler, Kirk, away from the wrapped presents beneath.

10,000 VOLTS

In late August, when Kirk was six months old, the four of us took off for The Ward Ranch, three hundred and twenty-two acres of redwoods on the Russian River. The ranch was two miles downriver from Monte Rio, on State highway16, twelve miles more to the Pacific Ocean. The very old dirt inroad was a bit over three quarters of a mile up the 1500 feet of elevation to the ranch house flat.

As said elsewhere, so many structures both on the ranch and our homes in Berkeley were built of redwood milled, on the ranch by my Grandpa Louis Ward.

The ranch house was three stories tall. The first being for normal daily living; the second three bedrooms and Grandpa's work study; and the third for family and guests. Two upright pianos, on the first and second floors.

The footage on each floor was 1800 square feet. Each of the three floors had their own beautiful used brick fireplace ... the only heat the building had available. Plenty of wood.

Our family/guest third floor had a complete kitchen area, bathroom, two bedrooms and quite an area of bunk space.

On that August visit in 1958, the four of us and my two nieces, Sharon (SALTU) and Kathy and their mother shared that third floor.

The story I want to tell here is: first thing one morning it was my turn to fix and feed four-plus months old Kirk's bottle at dawn.

The electric heating plate was taking and unusually long time. I leaned against a window looking east while checking and wondering what was taking so long?

Again, leaning against that window, I became aware of a constant buzzing sound. Looking around the room area, nothing. Back at the window with the buzz much louder there, I just happened to look down and see a high voltage wire burning through the limb of an apple tree in the orchard area below the power lines.

Thank Her that the heavy ocean fog had made much morning dew an event to bear at this time of year.

No phone!

I woke everybody while running down to the old ranch red pickup (a Jeep truck) and flying down that three-quarters mile of rutted dirt road to the Sheridan Ranch house just outside our Highway16 entrance gate. The time was now about 06:10 so I woke the Sheridens who helped me call both The Sonoma Fire Department and PG&E.

Then back up that rutted dirt road as fast as the Jeep could make it. There I found everyone safely huddled in the house.

Within less than five minutes of my getting back a PGE service truck roared up with lights flashing. The worker, from a distance surveying the scene told me, "I was the one who killed that circuit down below, but I won't go anywhere within thirty feet of that pole. We'll wait until the big boy crew gets here." To me, "man you're lucky as hell you did the right thing. This was just about ready to be one hell of a forest fire. One hour later, the dew drying the area?"

The big crew arrived and neutralized the area by driving a six-foot steel stake deep into the ground and did what I then learned was truly 'grounding the circuit.'

Before reconnecting the two lines with a simple clip, the crew chief showed me what had caused that almost disastrous break: there was a bullet nick causing it. When wires swung in the wind, the nick caused the wire to break.

Immediately realizing how this happened, I cornered Gwen, late sixties ranch caretaker, with the information that her two mid-teen summer helper boys had likely caused it. The second floor bedroom window looking at the last power pole in our system was the most likely spot for those boys, with their 22's to shoot at birds sitting on those wires.

Peacefully and quietly safely back home, my increasing work with Jimmie, Denny, and Hoyt kept us safely well afloat with Jackie's great connections steadily growing.

Our third daily helper, the Wonderful Ruth Godfrey, was only daily at that time. Not live in until our Keith addition. (Came to find out much later that the job had been handed down from ladies of the same church group).

JANUARY 1960

The Los Angeles Fire Department dropped by one afternoon and had strongly suggested clearing out the slough that had fallen and built up from the twelve-foot-tall cut in the steep hill of our home's pad over the years. That, in case they had to get back there to fight a fire. The distance from the house to the base of the base of the cut was roughly eight feet.

We were caught, literally between a rock and a very hard place.

Oh well, I bit the bullet hard and built a 2x12x20'ramp with two overlapping conveyer belts around the side of the house and down to a rented five-yard dump truck on Verbena.

We were almost three-fourths finished when the Los Angeles City Building Department showed up. A jovial middle aged city engineer, with clipboard in hand informed me, "Now that you've worked on the hill, ya gotta bring it up to one-to-one code."

(Much later I came to realize that we could have appealed the City's order since we touched the slough on recommendation of the City's Fire Department).

Glen Dee cutting

Jackie Loading

Soooo, then we enlisted Jackie's cousin, Glenn Dee, who was in the Navy, stationed in San Diego, for his help. He jack-hammered the shale, then he, Jackie and I shoveled the shale onto the conveyor, which took it to a five- yard dump truck at our curb.

We finally ended up losing gravity to be able to reach our conveyors, so, last chance, I hired a small mini-dozer crawler, lifted up by a crane over the house and set on a ledge to start to get the city off our backs.

We paid Dee off with our beloved ratty 1947 Pontiac woody station wagon. I was doing well enough now to buy a great used Ford station wagon through Denny's buddy, a used car dealer, Carl.

A very surprising happening was when, soon after the finished hill conforming escapade, we found out that Jackie was again pregnant.

Again, meeting our ever faithful and loyal OB Paul, in the 6400 block of Sunset Boulevard, he just shook his head with, "Well, here we go again."

I turned to Jackie with, "So much for your wanting to wait five years, huh?"

At home that night, dinner just finished, she asked, "Okay, how are we ...?"

I jumped in with, "We've got to create more space. Been hassling this all the way home from Paul's."

She quizzically looked with, "You have ... is there an answer you'd care to share with me?" I walked to the kitchen doorway, turned with, "If ... I say if ... I ... we add a room above our small patio, it becomes a new bedroom. Below, a new space for me to work. A twelve by fourteen area with a pull-down desk."

As she put the dinner dishes into the sink, "But what ...?"

Ignoring her interruption and continuing with my thought, I clenched the door jamb and turned to face her. "So... what if we create enough space for Ruth to live in? Save her bus fare. Give her weekends off to do her thing at her church rather than the usual Thursday maid's day."

Stopped in her tracks, "David, David, Ruth is no maid. She's so much more to us here that ...." She stopped short, "Agreed. For sure. Totally agree."

It took less than a month for Roger Farris, a contractor, and me to add the space for Keith and Ruth to live in. The three steps up for entry were at the end of the balcony on which Janice had stayed, bed ridden, and now into the new bedroom.

AN INTERESTING EVENT

One afternoon, a meeting in an empty recording booth at United Recorders with Hoyt, Jackie and four other singers. (By this time in his career Hoyt had been working heavily with Hannah-Barbera Productions).

Cliff Robertson and his wife, Dina Merril, and I are there in the background. What for? No idea.

Hoyt addressed the singers with, "I just want to make sure you all understand what we might do here today. This pilot bit shouldn't take over a half an hour for which you'll each be paid five hundred dollars. In other words, a buy-out. As you know, a pilot has a fifty-fifty chance of never being picked up. If it isn't you'll never hear it again. If it is, you may hear it for a long, long time. If you agree please sign these releases here."

They all signed and the recording of the main title for The Flintstones happened.

Just another way it worked. One of the lesser-known male singers, a few years later, tried to sue Hannah-Barbera. Nothing. But over quite a period Hoyt used Jackie doing solos for many commercials and voice-overs for several Hannah-Barbera characters.

AUGUST 4TH, 1960

It's now late in the afternoon and rather than rush everything, and "why not check into Hollywood Pres and relax?" Paul had suggested.

The nurses entered her room and implanted an I.V. in her left arm and then taped that arm to about an 18" board. Then we watched TV not having been told another part of their plan.

Nothing happened by midnight and Jackie was having trouble trying to sleep with that left arm aching. I'd fallen asleep on the small couch across from her bed.

Finally, finally ... finally, after the morning sun happened on the 5th of August, the Baby Delivering Crew started showing up. One of them opened a drip valve further and Jackie was now falling deep into the birth pains process for this day.

I did hear from one of those ladies that Paul had shown up, fully rested and ready to go to work. As upset and surprised by this totally different birth procedure both of us were, the outcome was successful and that, in the final analysis is all that really mattered, huh?

The second set of left-over D's; Dennis Keith Perry Ward arrived here safely. (By the way, must mention somewhere that, as I understand from one of my children, that Jackie has the four 2'x2' pre-delivery negatives of each of my four that Paul gave me after our final OB event ... yet to happen).

Thank Her that we added that new bedroom for now live-in Ruth and Keith. Robin and Kirk had more fun tending this newest addition. After a very few months, Keith, while on a soft blanket on the floor of my new office, started trying to crawl on the floor. After a few days of trying, he finally could make it off that blanket and now needed much closer tending.

Wish I really knew the months old he was when we put him in Kirk's old four-wheeled walker so he could strengthen his legs by walking and follow the other four of us around that ground floor.

After several fun months of that, I took him out of that walker hoping he would/could walk. He just went back to crawling again. Watching this for a few days, I came to realize that the walker had a front holding bar that he maneuvered it with. Was that what he was missing?

So, I took an old broom handle and cut it to about 18 inches and handed it to him. He stood up and walked holding that broom handle.

I'd started filming all of their history since Robin's birth. Robin and Kirk under the Christmas tree up through Keith while we lived at Verbena.

A morning in late 1962, Jackie and Ruth were working around each other in the small kitchen, fixing breakfast.

While checking the eggs in the smoking pan on the stove, with a sudden grimace she said, "Something's wrong, Ruth. Something's going on with me. I've been feeling lousy the past few mornings ... and ...."

With concern in her voice, Ruth ventured, "Hey, you're not working today dear lady, what about ...."

Overhearing part of this conversation while I was working in my cave, I moved into the kitchen doorway asking, "Overheard you two. So, what's goin' on?

Setting a dirty bowl in the sink Ruth faced me with, "You have time to see our Dr. Reichle today? If not, I'll see she gets there."

Back yet once again back in Paul's ever so familiar working space, Paul says, with a deep sigh, 'Well, here we go again." Hugging her, "I seem to remember you wanted to wait five years to have children?"

We just exchanged negative looks.

Later that day, Ruth was doing laundry while we confronted this surprise issue at the small custom built-into-the-wall eating/working table.

I took and patted her hand, "Okay, I know you're unhappy ... much more to put up with than me."

Looking off, she spit out, "Damnit! I'm so busy these days. So many great things are happening ... for us both right now. This is going to screw everything up."

Retracting my hand and looking off to Ruth working around the area, "I'll sure as hell tell you one thing; this has made this house, in this hilly canyon, way too small. No more room to add."

Getting off her stool and heading toward the living room, sighing a huge, sad sigh she reckoned, "I'd like to talk to Paul about other options."

I exchanged looks with Ruth and hung my head.

In his office once again, Paul, leaning forward from his desk chair, a very deep sigh and, "Well, dear ones, if you're even close to considering an abortion, sayonara. We're done. Great knowing you ... and thanks so much for your wonderful business."

Looks are exchanged in total silence as those final words sink in.

A couple of days of very few words while I started gathering possible new larger home sites and locations for us.

We agreed that we'd like much more space. Very tired living in a five cornered lot with only a shaved hillside of only semi-vertical space to look at, not really useful for what will become four kids. The loveliest place we found was way out Highway 101 at Lake Sherwood. Famous cartoonist creator Walter Lantz's home, right down to the water level.

Jackie's overwhelmed enthusiasm was voiced, "Gee, wouldn't that be a great place to live? The kids would really love it."

"Oh, do I ever agree, but ..." slowly facing the negative truth, "... the freeway doesn't come out this far yet. In two years, it might ...."

Slow to see my point, "I'd have to hangout in town if I had more than one session on a day." Making that long trip back into Hollywood, 101 was under extreme reconstruction for a good part of the way.

A much more practical lovely home I found was in Toluca Lake section of North Hollywood. It was on one and a half acres on Moorpark Drive on a slightly higher level looking into Bob Hope's five-acre pad with its pitch and putt area.

The home we liked had a four-car garage, and a lovely swimming pool area. The property was perfect for entertaining and close to most of both our work arenas.

Problem: Un-fixable problem: Only two bedrooms.

So, it took a little more than a month to locate the right house in an area I'd known so well: 144 N. Van Ness Avenue right in the wonderful old Hancock area of the Wilshire District.

Forty-one hundred square feet, five bedrooms, one being Ruth's right off the lovely family room. Even my John Burroughs Junior High School ex-girlfriend still lived at 123 S. Van Ness. (She and her husband were very good friends with Ronald Reagan).

As Jackie smiled, "Much better location. Five minutes to Paramount Studios and ten to Capitol."

"Also, I added, my brother, Roger, and I both went to Van Ness Grammar School, just across Beverly Blvd and up two blocks. Our homewreckers could even walk to school."

So, we bought it.

It was quite easy to talk both Ruth and Jackie into the plan for moving I'd worked out. After escrow closes, take a month to slowly take wagon loads to the house while contractors did some adjusting to bring the house into a bit better shape.

I did some work, too. When I got out of the service after WW2 ended, I worked for a little over a year helping my older friend as a lath and plasterer. The living room ceiling in our lovely new pad was old plaster with several large cracks that I just couldn't tolerate. But I could fix.

An important hangover, when Denny, as a Canadian citizen, had to leave the States due to the divorce laws, he'd left his cherry 190 SL Mercedes stored in our garage. In advising him of our forced need to enlarge our living space, we asked for his wishes on the 190 SL.

Since, in London, there was almost no use for a car, he asked that we ship it to him since the same Mercedes would cost twice as much there and he would then stable it in the country for trips over into Europe to visit his then wife, Lenita's family. This was accomplished.

Ruth would pack up all the kitchen ware we rarely used, and we'd take it to Van Ness and stow it away possibly, to never be used again. Same thing with clothes and tools. The very last load to move, I rented a trailer for the beds. That was how easy and simple our move was.

Some wonderful years passed when I had become so busy, dealing with our Big Bear Ward's Hardware mistake (more on this later) plus the 36' Teri-L headache (more on this later, also) that I needed more space within which to have a crew...if a very often deadline emergency was dumped that I'd eventual matured into needing more space.

1963 WONDERFUL SUMMER STORY

On the southwest corner of Vine and Selma streets, above the California Bank were three office spaces with a foyer which I shared with two other busy copyists; from the old Bandstand days, Roger Farris and the old Cameo days, George Tipton. On that second floor, was also Black radio station KDAY. George was later to become well known for his great work with Harry Nilsson. Wonderful Harry would spend many minutes of almost every day with us there before going off to his computer night job in a bank somewhere. We friends were privileged to be at Harry's very simple in-house wedding over off Beverly Boulevard and several houses south on Oxford Street.

Also using our office area as a major meeting and organizing front space were arranger/composer Perry Botkin, Jr and his lyricist, Gil Garfield. (They had several hits performing as The Cheers and then The Fraternity Brothers). They are the ones I mention since this story is about one of their/our hit songs.

(Also, must explain here: Perry Jr had only been known to us as Bunny ... all six foot three of him. This is because his famous father, Perry Botkin, Sr. was Bing Crosby's guitarist and very close friend and Bing named him Bunny).

Oops! Forgot to mention my wife, Jackie. She would hang out in our office if she had time to kill between singing sessions in that general neighborhood.

She just happened to be with us when this particular story started about the end of the first week in July 1963 and into the second week.

Jackie was in the middle of her ninth month of our fourth pregnancy (can't we wait at least five years before ... for the last time).

Harry was there dealing with George when Jackie came in and said to me, "Hey, all done for the day. How about some lunch?"

As George, Harry and I were getting ready to take up on her late lunch invite, the front office door burst open with Bunny and Gil immediately appearing. Seeing Jackie, Bunny erupted with, "It is just meant to be. Don't have to go and find you."

Grabbing her arms, "Dear, dear lady, can you do a quick demo for us at Gold Star for Gil and me? Just gotta hear this."

Shortening the story a bit, George and Harry went to Nickodel's for lunch while Bunny, Gil, Jackie and I went to Gold Star Studios for them to uncover their latest sensation.

In Studio A, Bunny pounded out the melody of their creation on the piano while Jackie looked at his lead sheet. He was belting out something like for a stage production.

She just started laughing, almost uncontrollably. "Bunny, you've gotta be kidding? This lyric is for a fifteen-year-old girl going back to school after a wonderful summer romance vacation."

She then started slowly singing her soft version and Bunny joined in on her soft tempo on the piano.

In the booth, behind the glass wall, that great audio engineer, Larry Levine started applauding. The demo was made in two takes. Bunny then grabbed the demo disc and with Gil, disappeared out the back door of the studio and of Gold Star Studios.

Jackie and I were now back in my office when Bunny came roaring in, just up Vine from Dot's office, about a hundred yards down Vine Street and above Music City at Sunset and Vine.

"Gotta have a session right away. Both Wink Martindale and Pat

Boone were in Randy's office and heard the demo. Wanna release ASAP. Tonight?"

Bunny then rushed out to write a lead-sheet arrangement and called four of the Wrecking Crew who were available. He also had to create a useless B-side "Dream Boy" for the record. Carol Lombard, Glen Campbell, Leon Russel, Hal Blaine and Bill Pitman all played on the track.? Find contract?

Fun memory: Engineer Larry talked me into playing on the final take. Overdub hitting a glass ashtray with a metal spoon for eight bars of after beats on the bridge. My only claim to actually being a recording musician for Musician's Local 47 Union. (no pay, though).

The record was done for the first time the next morning. Then Larry Levine's brilliantly mastered master was delivered to Dot within an hour and Wink took a copy to KFWB to start its new real life's exposure to the world.

Wonderful Summer Cover

KEVIN FINALLY ARRIVES

It was still very dark at 04:33 on the morning of August 14 when I was gently awakened by a fully dressed charming, beautiful lady singing, "Come on dear, wake up, the time has come. My water has finally broke n... for the first time. So, I think we'd better hurry? I've let Paul know ... and the hospital, too."

It took me less than a minute to dress and head down to the car where she was patiently waiting with the engine running. At that hour of the morning the Friday traffic was very light, and it took a bit less than twelve minutes to reach Sunset and Vermont where Hollywood Presbyterian Hospital was stationed.

Going around to the ambulance entrance, as dawn was breaking, a nurse, with a wheelchair was waiting for us.

While getting Jackie into the wheelchair the nurse informed us, "Dr. Reichle figured how long it should take you to get here. He just hopes he'll be able to make it in time."

The nurse then pushed the chair right past the admissions desk saying, "No time for that right now." Reaching the elevator and pushing the bell, she faced me with, "when we're safe and set and under control, you can come back down and take care of the paperwork. The chief resident is all set up and ready to go."

When the elevator reached the maternity delivery floor and stopped, the doors opened to meet a doctor and two nurses with the anxious doctor leading off with a smile, "No time for cordial introductions now. Dr. Reichle is about ten minutes away right now. Hope he makes it in time."

Waving me off, "please go get some ...."

I grabbed Jackie's arm, turning the chair slightly to give her a kiss. "Have a good trip?" She just squeezed my arm as the team moved on and I moved back into the open elevator and continued down to the admissions desk to complete my necessary duties. I then checked my watch against the clock on the wall behind the desk which registered 05:52.

In the father's waiting area, I was alone. That wall clock now said 06:21. A sudden shock when over a speaker system Paul's voice said, "Hey David, come on up."

I made my way back to the delivery area as a nurse came through the swinging doors carrying the bundle. "Mister Ward, meet your new son."

I was mentally stopped cold, "Son? No... no...you've gotta be..."

Really grinning, the nurse then opened the blanket to prove her statement.

"But ... oh hell. I've spent the last six months or more watching her get ready to have the girl she wanted so badly. She'd said, this time I want to do it right. She found all the wonderful custom dresses both grandmothers had made for Robin and all we ever thought about was possible girl's names and which one we were going to call our little girl."

All of that while the nurse led me back to Jackie's room and put our third boy back in her arms. She kissed me and then him and said, "Well lover, what boys' names do we have left?"

DEALING WITH INSIDE DAISY CLOVER

After the simple job Jackie did dubbing Hank Mancini's "The Sweetheart Tree" for Natalie Wood in *The Great Race,* she was called again to sing for Natalie in *Inside Daisy Clover* in 1965. This was to be quite a different project, this time, requiring weeks of work. *The Sweetheart Tree* took less than an hour.

> *Note: We intended to have a still from the movie The Great Race here, showing Natalie Wood lip singing the song The Sweetheart Tree, which was actually sung by Jackie Ward. The caption would have read: You see Natalie, but you hear Jackie. Warner has so far not bothered to get back to us about the rights, and the publisher won't use the picture without permission.*

Working for many years as a music copyist, having worked on record sessions, TV shows and film scoring sessions, I had worked with most of those in the Hollywood business of music.

Jackie, having no need for an agent—except for commercials—I

asked Don Williams, Andy's older brother who was his agent, to nego-
tiate for Jackie.

Don: "You do it, David. You know just what Jackie needs."

I tried to talk Charlie Stern, her commercials agent, into doing it. "I
only handle commercial artists, David. You do it."

Failing all other less than brilliant avenues, I gave up and decided to
do it. I hated the idea of negotiating ... especially for my wife.

So, I then contacted several of the great dubbing singers I knew so
well.

First one: Jimmy Bryant, the voice of Tony in "Westside Story" in
1960. Jimmy was great. "I had no idea what was expected of me. How
much time they bought for a flat $365 a week. Sitting around MGM for
way too many useless hours. Rehearsing was great. Marni was wonderful
to work with. So damned professional. One hell of a musician, too. The
number of singing calls I had to turn down and just wander the MGM
lot would make me aware of what I'd missed out on financially. Jackie's
so big with commercials and recordings sessions now, if I were you, I'd
be careful as hell as to how demanding they are of her time at Warner's."

Next came Marni Nixon. She had similar thoughts. Being Natalie's
voice in "West side Story," Deborah Kerr's voice in "The King and I,"
and Audrey Hepburn's Eliza in "My Fair Lady," as well as other jobs, her
advice was also, "you know what Jackie needs! You do it. Jimmy Bryant
is sure right about them wanting to own your life."

B. J. Baker, Jackie's buddy and being in the same vocal range, being Jackie's very friendly main competition for some jobs, told me that
"you'd better do it, David."

With all that investigation from the cream of the singer's studio crop,
I decided to try it. If I couldn't cut it, I could just walk out?

Having known Andre Previn since our John Burroughs Junior High
School days, and that Andre and wife Dory were the composers of this
film, I felt there might be at least some support ... some consideration.
We had also worked on several film scoring projects over the past years
together.

Warner's Music Department called and asked for a meeting to work out details so they could move forward with this part of the project. I was told that Sonny Burke, the head of the Music Department was ill and that a 'Joe McDonald would handle the meeting.' I'd worked with Sonny when he was the head of Decca Records. A hell of a lot more reasonable fellow. The meeting time and date were agreed upon.

The Music Department at Warner's was a lovely bungalow set apart on the lot out of the shadows of the tall stages ... right across from the commissary.

I fought to load all the nerves I could find ... from everywhere. Remembering Jimmy Bryant's encouraging words as I entered the bungalow's open door on that very nice bright sunny day. There, alone, was McDonald. A man in his early 60's, a skinny, about 5' 8" stern looking man. A firm, non-smiling handshake. He motioned me to an overstuffed chair in front of the desk while he took an executive-looking swivel chair behind the desk.

Referring to the plan I'd laid out after my research, I could tell he was not happy with my demands.

First: On rehearsal days, piano only rehearsal days, if Jackie got a very important call for a commercial or a session, with 24 hours' notice the rehearsal would be moved to a better time. McDonald, "No way. This can't happen. We never work that way. This is Warner Brothers. We don't move our schedules."

He tried to intimidate me with all sorts of tactics. "We can get a lot more, better singers in here and ...."

Moving on, I said, "When Andre and the orchestra are set, those schedules will be met. Any call-backs after the original scoring sessions are for an additional fee." Jimmy Bryant warned me about that one. "They own you until the film is 'wrapped.'"

After about forty-five minutes of bearing up under his insults, "who the hell do you think you are," etc., he finally picked up the phone and called somewhere in another building.

"You gotta deal with this dumb son-of-a-bitch. He's totally somewhere on cloud nine." With that he slammed up the phone. Almost snarling, he snapped out directions, "The producer, Alan Pakula wants to see you. He's in his office in that building," pointing, "upstairs, room 25," with which he turned away. We did not shake hands.

As I crossed to the building indicated by McDonald, my thoughts ran to, "I guess it can only get worse from here on out."

I climbed the stairs and found room 25, knocked on the door. It was opened by a grinning Andre Previn and warmly greeted with a hug. I was in immediate shock. It was quite a large room with two levels, one step up. From the desk on the upper level, broadly smiling producer Alan Pakula came down to our level and Andre introduced us.

Flashing thoughts: 'What the hell is this? What am I in for here?'

"David, so great meeting you,' Alan offered. "Looking forward to working with Jackie. Andre's really pleased, also."

Stammering, I started with "I thought ...."

"While you were coming up here, Andre and I spoke with McDonald and he told us the deal you two had reached. All is great."

Andre, "That piano rehearsal change bit is a great idea. Jackie's in too much demand to be tied up all day here for weeks."

Alan, "I'll have the contracts drawn up, sent to Jackie and you. Review them and if they meet your requirements, sign them and we'll begin. If not, make corrections and we'll get together again."

Such a great relief. After all the hair-raising trauma created in the bungalow down below, I drove home, not believing how relaxing and great Alan and Andre were. Nothing to deal with at all. What the hell, they could care less. They got what they wanted. So did I/we.

Jackie was so relieved since she had to put up with all my sweating out different scenarios for the weeks past.

I took her to the first piano rehearsal on the Warner's lot. The pianist was Harper MacKay who we both knew. I'd worked with Harper many times over the years on recording sessions. Natalie was also somewhere there. Within minutes, Alan showed up and motioned me to talk outside. As we walked across the lot, he said, "sorry, David. Natalie doesn't want you at these sessions. Is there something else you can do while they're working?"

"I drove her." A moment of thought. "About how long is this scheduled for?"

"Can we call you when they're close to wrapping?"

"Sure. Okay." At home. Twenty minutes from Hancock Park to here, traffic dependent. I have a cue for a Stu Phillips session for tomorrow I can work on at home."

A pat on the back, shake of hands and we parted.

Later, at the first orchestra scoring session, Natalie wasn't there so I stayed for a while. Andre told me, "Those people in the booth are so damned slow. They committee-debate so much it costs a small fortune in overtime. We don't need these three sessions scheduled for this film. Jackie's totally ready."

There was only one call back: to fix the scene where Daisy falls apart in the Circus recording session, for which she was paid, as was fought out with McDonald in the beginning.

ERROL WARREN EVENT

For some reason, in 1964 Jackie and I were in San Francisco without our family. We stayed with my dad and his wife, Angela.

Jackie had said that the only part of San Francisco she'd ever seen was the Mission area because that's where Dad and Angela lived. So, Dad suggested that we tour, even crossing into Berkeley to show the house where I'd been born. The house was all redwood lumber milled from our ranch as was Grandpa Ward's home. We rode the Bay Tour getting over to Alcatraz Island for a short tramp around it and then out under the Golden Gate Bridge to the Farallon Islands.

At lunch it hit me with, "Dad, one of the things I'd really like to do is visit The Court. I've heard they are moving it very soon."

A big smile and, "That would really be a great visit."

Just after his divorce from my mother and he'd been fired as the night editor and reporter from the Oakland Tribune for being one of the three reporters creating The Newspaper Guild, so, The Judge, my Mother's father got Dad on as bailiff of the Supreme Court. Ergo he had great interest in re-visiting his old work venue.

When we entered the Court Building at 350 McAllister Street in The City, we were the only people in the office and the current bailiff seemed quite annoyed when he had to tend to us.

He asked, "May I help you?"

Dad quietly asked, "What Justices might there be here today this afternoon?"

Now a bit more annoyed, he named four of the Justices in their offices, naming Justice Ray Peters as one.

Dad beamed, "Would you please tell Justice Peters that Estolv Ward would like a minute of his time to say hello?"

Now close to hostile, he motioned us to the long bench seat along the opposite wall, "Have a seat while I ask him."

It was a very short wait when he returned with a totally changed attitude. Now, almost graciously, "Mister Ward, Justice Peters asked if you could please, please wait for about fifteen minutes so he can clear his desk?"

When that wait was over, and we were ushered into Justice Peters office, we passed the open double doors leading into the Chief Justice's desk area. I paused Jackie to show her Fafa's office—where my grandfather served as chief justice. I gathered that the bailiff was impressed that I knew what that scene was.

An extremely warm hand shaking with Dad as he introduced Jackie and me to Mister Justice Peters. Quite a bit of recalling their admiration of each other's work history when Justice Peters told us a fascinating personal story.

"It was Saturday afternoon when I got back home after a round of golf. Kinda odd that my wife had martinis ready before my shower and dressing for tonight's big social event. As I was dressing and enjoying a second martini, she said, 'Ray, you're going to hear that President Eisenhower has just appointed Earl Warren as Chief Justice of the Court.'

Justice Peters then went into describing his reaction to this shocking news. "How could anyone make Errol Warren anything that legally high? We all knew the games he played from Alameda County District attorney all the way up to Governor. Then, for him to become the second greatest Chief Justice to Oliver Wendell Holmes was a mind blower for us all."

After a reflective pause, I came out with, "Well, Mister Justice, don't you think that when he'd reached the top of the tallest ladder in the legal land that he'd become untouchable? Who in the world would try and push his buttons anymore?"

With a huge smile, he stood, shook my hand with, "Wish I'd have said that."

While having a snack at SFO, waiting for our flight home, Dad brought up the most interesting proposition I'd had in most of my life.

"We've come to the realization that by adding a few more dollars a month to our retirement income we'll make our time left much more relaxed." Putting down his knife, "We'd like to offer the ranch to you, keep it in the Ward Family, for sixty thousand dollars. That would do us fine and give us great peace of mind also. Just so much a month is all."

A look at the two of us as we were amazed with this offer.

I took Jackie's hand with a squeeze as she beamed her accepting the great idea.

A shake of hands all around was all that was necessary to seal that tremendous bargain.

BEATLES KILL THE RECORD BUSINESS IN FEB 1964

The Wonderful Summer single got to number 14 on the Billboard charts but number one in most major markets. Held number one on the KFWB List for weeks. Dot Records gently pushed us to get a follow-up album ready. Since our K3 was born less than a month after finishing the single, which reached its top sales in October that we didn't think we'd have enough time to create ten more sides for release for Christmas. We did plan to have it ready by mid-December which pleased Randy Wood of Dot quite well.

I got buddies Jimmie Haskell and George Tipton to do four arrangements which left only two for Bunny since the single and its "B" side Dream Boy were in the can already. Jimmie and George's arrangements were almost sensational. Three absolute follow up hits for Robin Ward. (Jackie called herself Robin, after our daughter, for this project, because the songs were written for a young singer.)

Record sales except for artists such as Elvis, Welk and a couple of others died after the Beatles appreared on the Ed Sullivan TV show of February 9th of 1964. This shock was because five record companies had a backlog of Beatles songs they couldn't give away until that night.

Why, you might ask, singles cost $.95. Five cents tax? A fan would go into Music City with five dollars and walk out with five Beatles songs. Our great Robin Ward Wonderful Summer Album never had a chance.

All new record releases were shelved for almost seven weeks with this music business disaster.

(Just yesterday, March 23, 2024, Amazon had our album for $159 while Walmart has it for $199.)

1965 GIVING UP SMOKING

After Thoracic Surgeon Doctor Elmer Rigby's endoscopy of me at Hollywood Pres Hospital that day in mid-February, 1965 I went on a crusade of giving up smoking. (His procedure was extremely easy, but it took over two years for my lugs to stop hurting).

I'd taken up smoking when I was seventeen and aboard my merchant marine troop ship headed for Okinawa with the Tenth Army.

Both my sister and brother were chain smokers. Due to tremendous cigarette shortages during the war they'd taken to rolling their own and stripping found cigarette butts on the street, stripping what's left of the tobacco and rolling their own.

Aboard ship, I could buy a carton of Lucky Strikes for one dollar once a week. My duffle bag started getting loaded after we sailed from Pearl Harbor.

Standing gun watch on my flying bridge, starboard side, rear 20mm at dawn and sunset every day became very boring, except for my large coffee mug. I needed something else to do? All those cartons of cigarettes for my sister and brother? Maybe I should learn what immense pleasure they get from inhaling smoke?

So, I gave in.

Now, after Elmer's very personal and inside info about Nat King

Cole dying that day; "I opened him up, one look and saw he was almost dead, closed him and the press told the world that his cancer had been removed and he was fine."

I became dead set on getting rid of my three pack a day habit. (Many days were thirty hours for me. Many ash tray dumps).

When our family wagon, with four kids, would make the four hundred-twenty-mile drive to our Ward Ranch on the Russian River, above San Francisco, I could handle that. Being there, usually for a week or more, I'd stay out of the three-story ranch house as much as possible to allow the smoking women their smelly space. Then the drive back home. Tough, but my plan must succeed?

Then the truth hit me like a bolt: when I sat at my desk to work, I found where and what my hook was: work ... working with my pens at my desk.

From my swivel chair at my desk, I took a long slow look at my work scene. Where the coffee cup sat. The large ashtray next to my coffee cup and six-pen holster.

I sat there for quite a long time creating a plan since I'd finally discovered the main scene of my addiction.

I finally picked up my cute, quite overused mini pipe which could hold a cigarette straight up when the cup was placed for that position or straight out when the cup was repositioned for straight use. Okay, I'm going to use this pipe, empty, in my mouth as an emotional pacifier.

My God, it did work. For almost three weeks, it worked, tough going but working. But, alas, gnawing on the empty plastic pipe stem finally broke it down and I was suddenly back facing my square one.

Frustrated and desperate that my life saving pacifier was now ruined, I jumped in our wagon and went searching for the same small pipe cigarette holder. Surprisingly, I found one easily. Getting it home and trying it out, there came another great shock. No pacifying taste with this virgin.

What to do? I paced in the family room for about eight minutes when the brilliant recovery scheme flashed in on me; smoke a cigarette or two using it to take away its virginity taste.

So, I got out our house vacuum from Ruth's work closet and, with a now lighted cigarette in the holder, turned the vacuum on and held the device so the suction of the vacuum smoked the entire cigarette down in about thirty seconds. A second cigarette finished the much needed/demanded taste required to get me through those last few days of cigarette withdrawal.

Never had the urge since that day, thank Her!

1965 MICHEL LEGRAND

After the *Inside Daisy Clover* negotiations I'd suffered through, about a month later, famous cast booker Georgia Stark called me with some offer I can't remember. What the project was I can't remember because, here I was being considered Jackie's agent.

Well, she quickly decided that I didn't really understand what she was talking about and hung up.

A few weeks later, while we were at lunch, just the two of us, rarely in the dining room when the phone rang on the kitchen wall, above the normal eating counter. Ruth answered and called out, "it's for you Jackie. They asked if you were here."

Jackie went to the receiver and within thirty-seconds hung up and started gathering her purse, keys and work case then running toward the front door calling out, "they want me at MGM right now. Probably BJ screwed up again. See ya."

Well, seems that it wasn't BJ messing up but that Georgia Stark, I assume because of my screwing up her call to me, the entire vocal group was waiting for Jackie. Michel Legrand demanded that the session couldn't start without his two primary singers, Sue Allen and Jackie Ward. Thank Her I was never put in that unqualified position again.

Sue, Michel and Jackie

1965 JOHNNY MANDEL AND SUNDAY AFTERNOON WITH TONY BENNETT

After quite a number of years working with Johnny Mandel, who I had met in the fountain just above and inside the gates of the Beachwood ultra-small market area, we worked together on all work not controlled by the studios.

One really fun story: Trombone player John told me about the time he wanted to play with Count Basie. Basie asked him, "Why would you want to play with an all-black band?" He quietly answered, "I want to play the book." He got the gig.

Working on some film of which I have no recall, at about two in the morning I went to pick up his latest pages, in Mandel's new Laurel Canyon pad. He'd moved out of Glen Green from where we'd, for several years, been working in the Beachwood Canyon.

Pacing in his utterly cool Mandel frustration, he handed me a score with, "gotta scene with dying elephants and the damned director wants music to go with it."

A very quiet moment and then I came up with, "hey, write the trombones at their lowest in like a wave of sound?" He was thrilled. Just wish I'd heard that cue.

Last of many possible Mandel stories, for this epic, one Sunday, Tony Bennet came down from his gig at the Fairmont Hotel in San Francisco to do one of John's great new songs, The Shadow of Your Smile at a two o'clock session at Columbia Records, just two blocks east down Sunset Blvd from my office.

With the usually very late John, and on Sunday, I had to get three more pens available for this expected panic.

Okay. We were ready for the worst, in my above the Vine Street bank office, the four of us. The Shadow score arrived, by messenger, about 12:30 when John called and informed me that some well-known ghost would be writing the throw away "B" side.

Totally not unexpected with him. The four of us dug in with the eight bar score pages as soon as the pages were divided evenly.

Sometime between one and one-thirty, the great percussionist, Victor Feldman called me with, "hey Dave, anything special for percussion?" I had the other three check their pages and they indicated a 'no.' So I told Victor, "Nothing special, Vic."

The Shadow parts were sent, by messenger, to Columbia just before one-forty.

Well, the throw away took us about a bit over two hours to get on paper. As the crew was packing up, I told them, "Get your bills in within a couple of days and thanks so much. Just wish it'd been fun."

I then took the throw away parts, with score, and delivered them to Columbia, those two blocks east of us.

Entering the studio with this large orchestra playing, I got ready to hand out the parts when the take ended. I then noticed that Victor was frowning nastily at me which made me realize that he was now playing only traps ... not percussion.

When the shit was wiped off the scene, I came to learn that, to start the session, they had to break into some other drummer's locked up set, go to Music City, two blocks west, for sticks before they could start recording. This, my last of many Johnny Mandel stories for this time.

The beginning of my simple 'one day' two-year divorce caused the film MASH to be done without me and I never worked with John again.

SAVING MAC

On possibly my last day to attend the hardware store before it was converted into Anderson's Smorgasbord, the highway, at the San Bernardino Mountains six-thousand-foot level, where the treacherous two lane Rim Of The World twelve miles over to the lake dam, in last night's storm had loosened rocks and boulders from the steep, thousand foot, sheer walls and the road was an almost impossible drive.

But the truck and I both made it. Must have been since her truck body was so high off the pavement? A car would have been thrashed.

I entered the almost empty store calling Sid out of the office to answer the door chime. With an astonished look, "Wow, hi! Surprised to see you... Major alert that the Rim of the World's closed."

Now, seeming to understand what I'd just gone through, "Closed? One hell of a lot of rocks and a few small slides. But ...."

With a puzzled look, "I thought the CHP had it blocked off."

With a brow-wiping-gloved hand, "Huh! Well, I'm here, Thank Her! Where's ...."

Now that the shock moment of my arrival has passed and, "I had to take Jack down the hill to lower elevation in Apple Valley. B's with him ... in a motel." He then handed me a note. "Here's where they are."

It had been a very long time since I'd been down the back route from

Big Bear and into Apple Valley, very winding two lane road but no rocks and snow. My Dodge 3/4-ton flatbed and I made in just under an hour.

Easily locating the motel in this very small highway stop, finding the room from Sid's note, I entered to find Beatta tatting while Mac struggled, really struggled to breathe. Beatta's cool attitude irritated me but, psyching the scene out, I rushed Mac into my truck.

When paying the motel, I asked the clerk for the fastest route to George Air Force Base in Victorville. We made that well over the legal speed limit dash to George AFB in a time I can't remember ... or care. (I would have welcomed a Highway Patrol escort).

At the Main Gate we were, of course, stopped by security The casual guard asked, "What's your ...."

As calmly as I possibly could, I yelled at him, "I've got a dying navy veteran of Pearl Harbor who needs ...."

That was all he needed. He points, "Two hundred yards, right turn to the hospital." If my truck could peel rubber, it did as I took off as directed.

In a rather stark military waiting room area, Beatta and I sat. She was not tatting now and looking extremely cool while awaiting results.

After some unknown time, a doctor approached us, removing his mask as he walked, approaching me. "Mister Ward?" I nodded. "I must say you saved this man's life. He would have died within a half hour of when we received him. You say he was ...."

I jumped in with, "Mac, we call Jack, Mac, was Chief Radioman on the USS Enterprise which was at sea when the Pearl Harbor attack happened. He piped all the reception of the attack throughout his ship."

Now, extremely appreciative, "Sir, a life really worth saving ... thanks to you."

After ten days of stabilizing Mac's system, he was then transported to the Long Beach Naval Hospital for further help.

OCTOBER 1967

Shortly after Mac's horrendous event, my great buddy, my Best Man, had to finally bite a bunch of bullets and leave Ward's Hardware in Big Bear. His being forced to leave just added piles to my list of failures.

Between my record dates and film scoring sessions, I had to use any spare moments to service the Teri-l, close out the hardware store and find a new self-operating tenant.

The Anderson's had a very small seating smorgasbord out on the entry highway into the village. Long, long waiting lines most days. All six of us Wards had eaten there as often as the waiting lines were not too long.

Bent was thrilled with my offering the about three times the seating space. And with all those tree living spaces above?

Major chore; emptying the hardware inventory into the huge warehouse out behind. They kept their small shop in operation while I made the conversions between my recording sessions. Running back and forth up that mountain, locating and installing all the new restaurant equipment. What I really did learn about the restaurant business.

It took well over a month to make the switch over. Not a day's business loss ... for them. For me, clearing the hardware store out the back door and into the warehouse behind took every spare moment I had between sessions. Thank Her that during those heart attack days, Jimmie kept me, almost daily, onto his schedule, so I could adjust my eight hour trips up the hill.

Among one of my many lost dreams, by the divorce, was about that smorgasbord conversion, I was about to create a frozen food locker, where Bent would package and freeze left over food each day and then, since we had a side road area access to our back door, people, vacationers, fishermen could drive up and buy frozen dinners to take home and zap.

The Kids on the Teri-L

THE TERI-L ADVENTURE

Sometime in those mid-sixties yet another physical and psychological problem was forced on me.

It was 00:30 in the morning in 1966 when I was at my desk talking with Jackie's great buddy, group singer Carole Lombard on the phone while I just kept on working, turning score pages. We were due to go to San Diego in the morning.

Laughing, "Naw, Carole, it's too much work and responsibility owning a boat that big, and Marina Del Rey is a long way from our home here and right now Basin A has just been finished and there are less than twenty boats in it ... in the whole damned marina, for that matter."

"Aw come on David. Jackie needs something like that, someplace to enjoy the kids and ...." I leaned back in my chair, put my pen in its rack, picked up my coffee cup with, "What the hell about Big Bear? That's a great place for her to relax. Our honeymoon was there. Our new cabin to decorate while I fight out the mess the hardware store is turning into. Now add a thirty-six-foot Chris Craft to my worries? Hell no. No way. Shit kid."

"You know Ian is an ace of a sailor and I will go to hold Jackie's hand and ...."

Putting the refilled mug into the microwave, "But, it's a hundred and thirty-six miles from the last buoy in San Diego to Marina Del Rey. The Teri-L holds one-fifty gallons of petrol and the broker said she spends one gallon for each mile."

With her harder sales pitch, "I know. You've told Ian and me this many times."

Just getting back to my desk, I made some sort of a cutsie voice with, "Get off it, Shorty."

Quick aside: A meeting with Carol and Sal Mineo and me on a different session with them recalling their having a great time of their working with 'Baldie' on The King And I with Yul Brynner.

Back to now: "Just think of Jackie? Think of the kids? Think ...."

Setting my fresh mug down by the open score I was working on, I sat down into my swivel and reflected. "One thing I have been thinking about is when I was in the Sea Scouts, in high school, and our crew took that sixty-two foot World War one, wooden round bottom sub chaser from Balboa to Santa Monica. We actually had to stop over in San Pedro for the night. She was only making six knots and we had to get to Pedro before dark since they lowered the anti-submarine nets or we'd have been stuck outside those nets until dawn the next day.

Now, with her stage active voice, "Aw, come on Davey. For Jackie and your four wonderful kids? Think hard ... Jackie needs relaxation. Totally different escape for her."

"Hell, Shorty, you just want that damned seasick trip tomorrow."

Before dawn, now down at the marina in San Diego, Jackie, Carole, Ian Freebairn-Smith and I are taking possession from the Teri-L yacht broker. As dawn broke the area was quite foggy and overcast.

The very cheerful yacht broker, along with handing us the keys, "Her tanks are topped off. One hundred and fifty gallons. That should easily get you to the new Marina Del Rey. Bon voyage."

We made our way down the inlet channel of that marina and found buoy number one and turned north at about fifteen knots. Ian set the auto compass and it took over. I had our Wonderful Summer album playing in the background.

Because of the fog, the sea is exceptionally calm and just barely rolling. Three dolphins started playing with our bow as Jackie and Carole laid forward, on the bow, watching them play with the hull and the water we were pushing away.

After about two hours I'd become concerned about the fog and that since we hadn't seen the shore line since leaving San Diego, so I questioned Ian.

"Hey E, I'd like ... I think we should head a bit in toward the shore for some visual sightings. Find out where in the hell we are."

Looking at the helm and auto-compass, "We're on course. See the auto pilot is working well and ...."

"Please humor me, Ian. Know you're a pro yachtsman, but, please, please humor me on this one. Let's see if the shore is really there?"

He then disengaged the auto pilot and turned ninety degrees to starboard. The fog thins and thins and thins until a shoreline appears. I'm overwhelmed with what I saw.

"Oh shit! There ... there is Balboa. Balboa channel less than two hundred yards." With a look of his losing command, "So?"

Now excited, "Gotta, just gotta go there. Up that channel. The channel we left in our Sea Scout ship left in nineteen-forty-four."

Ian reluctantly guided the Teri-L into Balboa harbor. The Harbor Patrol ship shot us down because there's too much white water in the Teri-L's wake ... meaning too fast.

We tied up at a re-fueling dock and all left for some needed shore relief.

Returning, we found that there were less than five gallons of fuel left. Later learned that the yacht broker was totally wrong: two miles per gallon? No. One gallon per mile.

That scare brought me to think out and realize that yachtsman Ian had his experience with sail boats. I instantly became master of the Teri-L.

Back at sea and arriving at Marina Del Rey as the sun was a dark sunset. The tremendous breakwater, boulder-bearing barges caused scary channel entry problems. Our running lights were of very little comfort. We had to avoid the tremendously long mooring cables of those barges who were building the opening breakwater to the new marina. Think we even scraped our hull on one when turning into her main channel. Thank God it didn't foul our screws.

As we were tying up in barren Basin A with only about twelve boats now in the new marina, We made it. Tough getting her into our slip in the dark, but we made it. From 06:10 this morning. We made it. She's secured. Tied her up tight as hell.

Over the following months I came to realize that when we'd leave Del Rey there was nowhere to go except Catalina. The Santa Barbara Islands and Hawaii were too far away for our power boat fuel.

And the maintenance was all up to me. A boat, sitting in water, tied up to a wharf over twenty miles from Van Ness needs a lot ... I mean a lot of care. Like, the beautiful red mahogany transom in the stern had to be sanded and re-varnished several times due to sun exposure. (Later realized I should have covered it with a tarp?) One hell of a lot of maintenance and a long way to travel to do it. Came to realize that if we ever owned another boat, it would be trailerable and sit in our back yard or close by.

Only once did Jackie and the Teri-L venture any distance: we dared to go to the Isthmus at Catalina, forty-one miles away. Eighty-two miles both ways. A half load of gas.

Much later met with Robert Wagner at a TCM Event and told him about our experiences of our trying to get into our dingy at the Isthmus of Catalina Island as well as Jackie voicing for Natalie in two films.

About a year before my fatal divorce, I sold half of the yacht to the great studio drummer, Frankie Capp. The first thing he wanted to try was fishing out beyond the breakwater. He was nattily dressed in yachtsmen's attire with a jaunty captain's hat covering his well-placed toupee.

So, we were fishing off the stern when he decided to move to the bow. "More room up there and less getting poles tangled."

Now, with pole in hand he started moving past the cabin roof on the 18" wide deck. There was a handrail on each side of the cabin roof to make this passage much safer. (Tied up in the marina no need to use one).

Frank was almost halfway there when a wave swayed our Teri-L and he was, at that instant, without a hold on the safety rail.

Quite a yell of, "oh, shit" and a huge splash overboard. Of course, the pole, cap and toupee were gone.

The freeboard (boat side above the waterline) was about five feet. My leaning over the side that far was extremely unwise, so I grabbed the nearest mooring line and threw it to him. Then I got the eight-foot folding rope ladder from the transom storage and put it over the rear and the leading him to that ladder.

That was the last time we went fishing together. I was having too many troubles with our Big Bear property to see much more of her. I understand that Frank became quite fond and enjoyed using her often.

NEW ORLEANS, JULY 1968

Sometime earlier that year Jackie was asked to represent the singers at the SAG-AFTRA Convention in New Orleans. It was the actor's year to work on their new contract negotiations, so the singers were free after the morning update session to explore and enjoy New Orleans fun area.

So, all five elected singers, four guys, Bill Cole, Ron Hicklin, Stan Farber, one more I can't recall, and Jackie took their spouses along to enjoy that legendary city from their lunch break until dawn.

Most days began with most of us for Breakfast at Brennan's, a New Orleans Must.

Then, while the members were tied up in the morning session, I chauffeured their ladies around scouting areas the husbands might want to see later. Five days of this.

One morning the four ladies and I tried crossing the twenty-four-mile-long bridge over the twenty-three-record breaking plus mile long Lake Pontchartrain Causeway.

We had gone about five miles out on that two-lane span when the wind and rain started ruining our adventure. I finally found a very small turn-about area and we all agreed, "Let's go have lunch when the rest are finished for the day."

Another morning, we crossed the Mississippi on the Huey Long Bridge and made it out onto the Louisiana Bayou area of Lafayette. Most enjoyable.

On our way back to the Huey Long Bridge, as we were driving on that remote moss-covered tree roadway, we suddenly looked up and out to see a large tugboat, on an elevated canal moving in our direction. I slowed down quite a bit so all of us could ponder that scene.

Each evening, with spouses, were events to remember for many, many years.

On our last day, when at Louis Armstrong International Airport, while the singers and spouses were waiting to board, Bill's wife came out with this, "This trip was so great. Such a fun time. We've gotta do it again next year."

Clapping her hands with gleeful approval, Stan's wife burst out with, "Yeah! For sure!" Making a hillbilly voice, "That's for dang sure."

A great reaction brought Ron's wife to add, "That's New York ... for sure, we've just gotta all make that one. Chew on some of that Big Apple."

Chuckles from all as some of their carry-ons needed adjusting.

Last to throw out her thought, Bill's wife, with a look of her possibly topping thought about to be aired, "Hey, we could make a one daytrip up to Boston? I have many great places to show you guys." The last voice that I remember commenting was Jackie's with, "It's a date ... that's for sure. That's for dang sure."

Returning home, the following days/months were flying by with work.

It was one hell of a year. Did two films for Johnny Mandel as well as two for Stu Phillips. Also work for Haskell two plus at least two record sessions each week.

EUROPE

Just after Christmas of 1968, I was copying some score at my desk, just between the family room and front room when the phone rang. Looking out into the family room and finding that Ruth wasn't around I picked it up with, "Hello?"

Calling was my longtime friend and musical client Bob Thompson. "Hi Dave, Bob here." "Well, hey, hi, Bob. What's up?"

"Well, you've been asking me about suggesting Jackie for commercials for a longtime. That last national spot you told me about has this thing moving."

Putting my note pen back in its holster, "Okay."

"Well, I have some major spots to do, in London, for the owner of the Baltimore Orioles baseball team just after the first of the year. You guys have any interest?"

Now really curious and attentive, "Okay, Bob, how high is the pile of shit you're piling up going to be?"

A long, huge laugh then, "Come on, Dave, this is for real. The owner heard Jackie's spot and said, 'get her.' That's where I am right now. You guys wanna go to London ... in three weeks?"

A very, very slow take to absorb the words of his offer. "Wow! Give me a minute to ... I can't totally commit until I check with

Jackie but a moment of dead silence then, "Oh, hell! You know Denny Farnon?"

Somewhat confused, "Sure. Denny was ... but ...."

"Well, he had to escape to England because of the California divorce laws. Being a Canadian citizen, he easily escaped the male commuting to a life of servitude divorce laws."

His confusion continues with, "Okay, so what. What the hell does that mean for this?"

I replied, somewhat joyfully, "Give me four minutes to attack what's left of this over-stressed brain to figure all this out. Shit, let me reach Jackie. No, wait until she gets home so we can figure this all out. Basically, it's an absolute yes. A positive 'Yes.' Can't imagine she's not all on board for this."

Now with it and back to business, "Well, we're booked at the Wellesley, in London, on January 10th for four nights. You figure it all out and get back to me ASAP."

With a total aside I muttered, "Oh, crap. Gotta figure how to reach Denny. Find out where he lives and ...."

Interrupting my deviation from the now question, "Okay buddy, get it all done. Luckily, he wants her. Timing, then, becomes more negotiable."

It was a bit after that evening when Jackie got home. The kids and Ruth were watching the family room TV. She put her satchel on the kitchen sideboard, opened it, took a contract out, looked it over and put it back, snapping the locks closed. Then, she turned and smiling, was about to address the children when I rushed out of my office and grabbed her with, "Hey, lovely, let's go out to the studio. We need absolute quiet with no interruptions for right now."

With a look showing her amazement and confusion by my insistence and urgency, I took her hand and made it out the back slider and up into my studio.

My very slow but highly informative explanation of what tremendous proposition was on our table right now, with multi questions and answers, we finally both agreed to what a great opportunity this offer was.

Preparing to travel overseas was a gigantic time scramble getting our passports issued. It generally takes six to eight weeks. I made an urgent request which brought ours down to two weeks.

Then we had to have a series of shots for international travel.

I was able to make contact with Denny and Lenita and they were thrilled. They booked us lodging at the ancient Royal Court Hotel just two blocks from them just off of Sloane Square in Chelsea.

For some strange reason I think that we flew on British Airways direct from LAX to London's Heathrow airport nonstop. We arrived at Heathrow about 04:20. Gathering our luggage onto carts, we made our way, following the crowd and verifying by the arrows, to the Customs Counters.

The uniformed, very polite British officer, while checking our passports, "Your reason to visit the United Kingdom?"

I answered, "We're here to work."

Immediately looking up from our passports, "Work permits then, please."

Now, after this long tiring flight I'm stunned for an answer. Totally lost, "Work permi .... Gee, what are they?"

With a very serious but politely answer he had to give so often, "Sir, to work in the UK you must have a legal work permit."

Jackie looked at me for a trip saving answer.

Possibly about to throw up, I barely could get it out, "Oh, my .... We're just here to record music created here for ..."

As he now stamped both passports, he smiles and, "I see. Thank you, sir." Pointing in a direction, "Please move on."

We're now lost deep in a very quiet Heathrow at 05:33 in the morning. I was pushing our luggage cart while searching for the next step.

Holding on to me quite tight, "Okay, what do we do now?"

Looking at all the empty booths at this hour, "We've got to get to our hotel in London as ...." With her most scared/lost voice she asked, "Do you have any idea how?"

That question caused me to come to a halt. Looking every which way while searching for the best possible answer.

A long, very deep breath and, "We've gotta get British money first. Can't move from here without it. We can't use dollars now."

We slowly moved ahead frantically searching for answers, when I spot an open Money Exchange Booth open, and we moved to it.

To the only clerk who's adjusting new inventory, "Pardon me but ...."

So obviously skilled in his work, "Hey, you need to change dollars into pounds so you can operate within the UK, right?"

A hearty yuck from him, then I asked, "Well .... Hey, how'd you know?" Shaking his head slowly, he just smiled even broader.

Finally, the important thought, "Hell yes. We need to get into London and ...."

Now to helpful business, "Well Mate, just tell me how much you'll need while you're here. If it's just enough to get into London, I'll give you that. When you're there and oriented, you can exchange more ... all over, almost anywhere."

I smiled at Jackie's grin as I could see she was relaxing some.

Pointing out a direction he said, "Take your Brit pounds, go to the bus depot around that corner and they'll be glad to lead you to the exact place you need to get to."

Our last expression of tremendous pressure release. Now beaming, in unison, "Oh, thank you so very much."

Offering his hand for a shake, "My pleasure. That's what I'm here for."

The bus depot was mostly full of the famous British double-deckers. Also a couple of single-deckers, which I later learned were for the long rural runs.

The station master, clipboard in hand, spotting us came to meet us and our luggage at first sight. He was a very happy looking man in, must have been his seventies.

"Where might we take you quite early birds?" he questioned with quite a thick Irish brogue. Checking my travel notes, I replied, "We're headed for the Royal Court Hotel" rechecking his notes, "that is supposed to be in the Chelsea area of Sloane Square?"

"Good." He then led us past three buses and informed the driver of the fourth one and his lady stewardess of our destination.

The bus stewardess then motioned us to climb the stairway to the upper deck while the driver stowed our luggage in the baggage space.

It was about ten minutes before we departed. About twelve more passengers boarded in the meantime. The bus, at that early hour of the day was hardly crowned so we got the front seats on the top deck saw, first-hand, the best view of the English countryside and then into London.

OUR BUS RIDE
INTO LONDON

As tired as we were, that wonderful ride was an event to always remember.

En route, the extremely kind stewardess offered us suggestions of how, when reaching Brompton Road, to grab a cab for the very short ride to our Royal Court Hotel. The Royal Court, in Sloane Square, we'd chosen since it was just around the corner from Denny and Lenita's home.

The famous Royal Court Theater was just across the street from us. When asking the concierge about the Royal Court productions, "So sorry, sir but highly advise that the Royal Court productions are very much too British for you, Might I suggest the Wyndham's Theater? Sir Alec Guinness is ...."

Stopping him short, "Do you mean, *The* Alec Guinness?" Seemingly impressed with my enthusiasm, he went on with, "Well, yes sir. Sir Alec is now appearing at the ...."

Interrupting him once more, "You mean, THE Sir Alec Guinness is on stage, working while we're here in ...."

Almost enjoying my interrupting enthusiasm, "Oh, yes sir at Wyndham's Theater he's doing *The Cocktail Party.*"

A moment of silence while I hugged Jackie.

Slowly, in anticipation of a negative response, "Are there seats avai ...."

"Oh yes sir. We can book them as soon ...."

Really beaming now, "Right now, please. Save us two seats for ...."

After a day of unwinding from the long trip, we went to the Wellesley Hotel to meet up with Bob and the owner of the Baltimore Orioles, Jerold Hoffberger to get the recording schedule.

Bob laid it out for us. "We have two days booked but," looking at Jackie, "we'll most likely get all the spots done before lunch. The six tracks are in the can and the vocal's lyrics are all just a slight variation of each other."

The four of us then had a very relaxing long lunch into the midafternoon. When Hoffberger left to answer some business phone calls, I asked Bob, "Okay, why does he come all the way over to the UK to record a half a day of commercials?"

"The orchestra can take up to four sessions in two days and he hates the American musicians' unions," was his answer. The one session was easily completed so we said our thanks and goodbyes to Hoffberger and Bob and the reason for the trip was now over.

The day we arrived we contacted Denny. We invited them to a posh dinner the night after the Hoffberger/Thompson powwow.

Lenita, after that expensive elite dinner out, having been embarrassed by us two ugly Americans and their dinner tipping had finally, after several dinners sessions, educated us to the fact that almost all of the UK and Europe that the menu price contains all fees. Taxes, tips and all. "Ya just lays the menu price on the table and walks out."

OUR EVENING WITH
SIR ALEC GUINESS

Our superb evening with Sir Alec Guinness at the Wyndham's theater was the following evening. The theater was only half filled. We had plush velvet seats center in the first balcony section. It was one of the greatest live theater experiences of my life. No. The greatest is still having Jackie in my life. Close second best this London Theater watching Sir Alec Guinness, live, on stage, in historic Wyndham's with subways noises running just below. A once in a lifetime thrill. At the first intermission white coated waiters came and took refreshment orders which were then delivered at the second break.

Since we were now restaurant-educated by Lenita, we ate in small places of their choice. In a small Soho café, we four had just about finished dinner when Lenita looked seriously at the two of us from across the table, "Please bear with me ... but Dennis and I have a possible plan we'd love to throw out to you."

Putting my coffee cup back onto its saucer, we were now both alert.

Sitting straight up and clearing her throat, "As you know we're in the immediate process of moving to my homeland in Portugal. I hope ... plan to get this major move over in at least the next ten days." taking Denny's hand, "What we'd love, if your time and schedule can let it happen, we'd love to have you visit us after our move is completed."

What a shock causing an extreme reaction from both of us. At last, stuttering, Jackie managed, "But, how ...." and she looked to me for help.

The surprise wearing off, I added, "Wow! Hell. Oh, wow! How would this work? How can it work?"

Later, on our way to our room at The Court, we stopped in the lobby and picked up many European travel brochures. We were up until the wee hours trying to work this great unexpected surprise, just dumped on us, all out.

I recalled, "She said that they needed at least six days before they'd be ready for us." Looking up from a French pamphlet, I suggested, "What about France for two of those six days?"

"But, the language and the money and ...."

"We can book in Hilton hotels. They've gotta speak American. Same for Italy." Now more with it, "And, and two more days in Rome?"

Overwhelmed, shaking her head, "Are you kidding? Oh, my God. How might we ...." Checking my watch, it showed 03:21 UK time. Thinking out loud, "that means its 18:21 yesterday Ruth's time. I then picked up the phone and called her advising her of our sudden change in plans ... home six days later than planned.

I'd decided to stick with British Airways since we left home with them. Never having traveled out of our country Jackie was hyper nervous. (I was too).

So, to calm both of us quite a bit, I came up with, "We should stick with the Hilton Hotels since I guess they speak and understand American."

The suggestion seemed to relax her ever more. I booked the Paris Hilton which was located within two blocks of the Tower Eiffel ... walking distance.

Denny and Lenita had friends in Paris who picked us up at Charles de Gaulle airport and on the way to our Paris Hilton pointed out major points of interest along the way. I also had oft wondered why European cars were so small. And, why an American Chevy sedan was such a limo over there: the ancient streets are so narrow and the parking almost impossible. Two for one.

We were treated to the Tower, The magnificent Louvre Museum, Notre Dame, The Opera House, up the hill to Montmartre, on our first day and to Versailles/Fontainebleau on our second day.

That night, goodbye to Paris, our two-day new friends, and on to Rome.

The difference in currency was a complete shock to me. Getting in the cab at Rome's Leonardo de Vinci airport, when the driver flipped down the meter switch it scared the hell out of me when the figure of 600 visually yelled out at me. In Paris one Franc turned out to be twenty cents: five franks equaled one dollar. Much calmed down a lot when I later learned that 600 lire equaled one dollar.

We were now totally alone there in Italy. No friends of friends to lead us through this entirely difference although both countries almost sharing the same border but for Switzerland.

Became somewhat disappointed to learn that The Caligari Hilton was nowhere close to the main parts of Rome. A free twenty-three-minute shuttle ride to the famous Spanish Steps area was needed for our two days of four tours. (But, in that time of January they were very tourist quiet but did speak American).

The American Express tour offices were located at the right side of the bottom of the wonderful Spanish Steps. One morning tour to the unbelievable Vatican and Sistine Chapel, then lunch. Then the afternoon tour to The Colosseum. Timing wise we were forced to meet the free time limiting shuttle ride back to The Caligari Hilton for a quiet, boring evening.

The second day of tours were historically art; very interesting. The part I liked best was standing under the Arch at the Head of the Appian Way. There we saw the starting point of where Rome moved for its conquering its foes.

Also, the buildings in that area were denuded with their marble coverings. Also, we learned that there still existed a very more ancient city below this area only accessible by tunnels.

Very early the next morning we were shuttled back to da Vinci for our flight on to Lisbon … with a flight change in Barcelona, Spain.

Arriving at BCN after almost two hours flying, we came to learn that our connecting flight to LIS was delayed due to bad weather conditions.

It was about 09:00 when we arrived. Around 11:30, some of the more worldly traveled passengers started booking alternate flights for varied different end locations and left.

After snacks, furnished by the airline, at about 14:00 we were advised that TAP Airline was going to try. Of course there wasn't an empty space on that aircraft. The two-hour flight was extremely quiet inside that passenger space. Only fog and rough air the whole flight.

When we started to descend, I checked my watch and knew we were going to try and land. With nothing but window fog, and not a sound except for those praying.

The wheels screeching rubber on the runway was our first clue that we had made it. The shouts of joy were impossible to describe.

LIS was now officially closed, due to the weather.

Lenita met us with a ride while Denny acted as babysitter for their two young ladies. As we moved closer to the coast, the weather cleared quite a bit. Driving up the coast toward their home in Cascais, the beach reminded me so much of the beach at Malibu except that train tracks were running along just below our slightly elevated roadway.

Again, greeting the entire family at dinner was worth the hazardous day's event. Listening to Denny's latest large orchestra music, while eating, was another relaxing pleasure.

Bright and early the next morning Lenita hauled us on the fifteen minute drive up to Sinatra, one of the most charming spots on this earth, for me. The spectacular Palacio da Pena stands out as it controls the top of that mountain. A second fun visit after an early brunch was the ninth century Castelo dos Mouros looking out toward the Atlantic Ocean a few miles away.

Love to go back sometime.

Our last day was spent shopping in Lisbon. I was lucky to have Lenita visit her father's boot maker. Would've never come up with that visit. He measured my foot and made me the best pair of casual loafers imaginable. He offered to make a last (model) of my feet and whenever I needed great shoes, no matter where I lived, he'd send pictures and he'd make them. Since my visit to him was the first thing that day, my most wonderful loafers were ready before returning to Cascais for our last night. On our third morning we were booked on TAP to fly from LIS to ORY, in France, there to connect with British Air for our eleven-hour flight back to LAX

1969 PLAZA RESTAURANT

One afternoon in March we went to a bite of lunch at the Plaza Hotel restaurant on Vine Street to discuss possible problems with Robin's growing up.

As the waitress collected the menus with our orders of two coffees and the snack tray, she left as Jackie asked, "Okay, do you have any ideas?"

Leaning forward I came slowly out with, "I think it's something we have to handle. Our parenting chores have been so easy up until now. Van Ness Avenue was no problem at all."

Now leaning a bit closer, "Sure, but how?"

With a big smile and moving back a little, "Hey, you're her mother ... and a woman ... and you went through your teens and came out the other end okay."

"But my teens were in Newman Grove, population one thousand and three and changing up and down every week."

With a big grin, "But, you were born in Hawaii."

Looking for the waitress, "Only until Pearl Harbor until I was seven. Then Newman Grove for my teens."

The waitress returned with our orders and placed them on the table and left.

"Well, Janice was born in Newman Grove and you saw how she went through her teens before you ...."

With a disgusted look, "Oh, crap! Please don't ruin my meal." Slightly shaking my head, "Wow! I can only imagine."

Picking up her coffee cup, "If Robin has the problems Janice had, I'd suggest sending her to a convent to protect her."

Looking at her straight on, "but she's only thirteen and has just started John Burroughs. Although, that's where I went to junior high, my memories of those years are what worry me." Leaning back a bit and picking up part of my sandwich, "And I was so stupid and naive I had no idea of what those girls had in mind."

Shaking her head, "I'm sure it was much, much different than Newman Grove Seventh Grade."

Taking a bite and speaking with a mouthful, "Well, yeah. We had almost four hundred in our class of '42."

Snickering, "What a hell of a comparison. That comparison really works, huh?"

With a deep, thoughtful look, "Ruth said that she's been getting home from school a bit later each week. Sometimes just before dinner. I've been keeping track and she's right."

Thinking heavily, she slowly said, "So, we might have a real problem. So, tell me, what might we do?"

"Well, I have been thinking and have come up with one idea."

Eagerly leaning back with a 'show me' look, "Okay. What a great idea for this?

"What if we play a game like Russian Roulette? After school Russian Roulette."

Her eyes squinting a bit, "What are you ...."

Taking her hand, "We set up a deal where whoever is available meets her after school. She's instructed that she leave the school by the front door. If she sees the station wagon out front, she gets in and goes home ... no matter what she and her buddies have planned. No excuses."

I can see that I've really tweaked her interest to hear more. "If one of us can't make it, Ruth gets on the Third Street bus and meets her outside. She never knows if anyone will be there and this makes any firm hanky-panky plans very hard to carry out, almost impossible."

Now totally with what my idea is, "Okay, but ...."

Talking right over her thought, "This only happens ... maybe once a week, maybe three or four times a week. Keeps her off kilter. Always has to wait 'til she checks the school front door on McCadden."

She now beamed. "That might work."

Feeling that I've made a good point, "Hey, it's a start. The only one we have now." We clinked coffee cups.

The calendar days are now flying by pushing between going back and forth to Anderson's Smorgasbord, now on Pine Knot Boulevard in Big Bear, to try and get my frozen dinner plan finalized before the vacation summer crowd invades the mountain once more.

It's now about the first of June when my phone rings. I leaned around the corner and see that Ruth's out in the back yard. I switched on the speaker and adjusted the score I was working on.

"Hello there."

Jimmie's voice answers with, "Morning, Dave. Hope it's good because it's going to get better ... right now."

"Sounds go, Jim. Better can only mean good news."

"Dave, going to do a pilot for the Doris Day TV show. It goes in two ...."

"What dates, Jim. I'm booked for the SAG-AFTRA Convention in New York ... hangover trip from last year's New Orleans gig. A bunch have planned to have a great time and ...."

A moment of silence and Jimmie comes out with, "Hey, you know who ever gets the pilot gets the show ... if it goes. I really want you to ...."

"Aw, hell, Jim, been on this for so many months that I can't let the gang down. You shoulda heard the plans they ...."

"You're sure? You're really sure?" he asked.

"Yep. I'm too committed to ...."

Sounding disappointed with his great news, he followed with, "Okay. I'll really miss you if this gig goes. Happy New York."

It's mid-July when Jackie and I finished checking our luggage in at the American Airlines counter and headed for the boarding gate.

Arriving at the gate, there were Stan, Bill, Bob and Ron ... all by themselves. I looked around and asked, "Hey, where are the others? Where are your ladies?"

With a very puzzled look Ron asked, "What others?" Bill also, "What ladies?"

Now I'm totally lost and feeling total panic building up within me. I came back with, "Well, the gang we ... last year we all planned to ...."

Sensing the tenseness growing within me, Bill, very slowly and precisely asked, "What are you ...."

Stan jumped in with, "Where in hell have you been, man?"

As we prepared to go through the boarding gate, Bill took my arm. "Are you serious ...? Didn't you know?"

Flashing his ticket to the guard who checks off his list, Ron, now with his most serious tone, "Dave ... Dave, this year is the singer's year."

"The year where we are it ...." Stan mumbled.

Totally lost on this cloud of confusion my mind darted to 'I wonder if Jimmie's started the Doris Day show writing yet. What if I ....'

Bringing me back to now as we walked down the boarding ramp, I heard, once again, from Ron, "This is our year, Dave."

Jackie had already moved ahead of us since I was slowing down while grasping for reasonable words to consider and say.

As we ducked to enter the ship, Bill added, "No fun. Just hammering out union negotiations. All day and deep into the night."

Taking my seat next to Jackie was hard to do. She just looked out the window putting an obvious wall up.

During our five-and-a-half-hour flight, history was being made on that July 20th, 1969: Neil Armstrong and Buzz Aldrin had just landed Apollo 11 on the moon. We watched it all happening on American's big screen.

After taxiing to and checking in at The Waldorf Astoria we were told that there was, in Times Square, an exact copy of Apollo 11 set up. It was dark now and the lighting of the LM made it well worth our effort.

That was the first of my several unpleasant trips to New York City. Just wandering the sights and meeting the singer's group for a quick dinner meal and then back to our Waldorf room to watch TV until Jackie came in, usually between 12:30 and 1:30 for each of the five days.

"And to think I gave up Doris Day for this?"

One very hot, sweaty day, I took the shuttle ferry over to Liberty Island to climb the extremely narrow and steep metal spiral steps to the top of the Statue of Liberty with a gals butt several inches in front of my face. Later wondered who was behind me?

Another normal horrible New York experience was when I had lunch at the Waldorf coffee shop. A waiter delivered a hamburger to me. I lifted the bun to find the empty bun with only a lonesome meat patty.

As the waiter again passed, "Wait ... please ...." He stopped cold and I asked, "Is there ... can I have some thousand island and a tomato and ...."

With a New York snarl he asked, "What? You from California? Want a garden all over it?" What I came to find out as usual with the locals.

On our escape from New York back to a home where I could understand life, the flight seat, next to me, was empty. Jackie now sat with our great buddy Tom Kenny. I assumed talking how the negotiations went.

At this point in my life's story, gotta set the stage: more of my back story.

Since the destined Ward's Hardware store failure, on Pine Knot, in the heart of Big Bear village had slowly, with much pain, both financial and personal disappointment from/with all those great people who ... who had lived this same dream with all of us, was converted into Anderson's Smorgasbord.

While this transition took place, I continued, when my business obligations made the time possible, to trip that tough route up highway330 and drive the now clear and open Rim of the World, to finish my last warehouse project: building a collapsible frame for my Dodge custom flatbed stake truck for my, from my late youth dream, a rough camping trip with my kids on my tarp, hay covered hard truck deck, then covered with a tarp for sleeping.

My idea was to relieve Ruth and Jackie for a couple of weeks of

relief and recovery for what's going to come up with them in the coming school year with our brood. Robin, now in my old junior high
school, John Burroughs. This was where life really began for most of
us, as teenagers. The dances and all the sex mixing events bursting out.
Unstoppable with each of the three years there before onto the worst of
the trials yet: high school.

After the fiasco New York mistake, at the end of July, out of nowhere, Richie Frost, Ricky Nelson's drummer, on the great Ozzie and
Harriet TV Show, since its creation, with the Malt Shop Group, was
quitting and wanted to move his family to Oregon for a different life.

Richie had a 26 foot Beechwood Motor Home with just over 6000
miles on it and was financed with our Local 47 Credit Union.

My paid-for Dodge Stake pick up with just under 10,000 miles blew
onto the scene. (No memory how, when).

So simple to do the financial work through our 47 Credit Union.
Easiest financial deal I'd made so far ... or, since.

At the very end of July, my nightmare of making the conversion of my
truck into a camper, now gone, my ulcer pains greatly reduced without help.

Our almost new Beechwood motor home now rolled merrily along
I-15, up and into and over El Cajon pass toward Victorville.

ROBIN, now 13, KIRK, 11, KEITH, 9 and KEVIN, 6 years are
fighting and establishing their individual territories in our new thrill.

My yearlong original plan had been to convert my oversized stake
bed three quarter ton Dodge truck into small camper much as the one
my John Burroughs Junior High agriculture teacher had done. A stake
truck with its deck hay covered, topped by a huge tarp on the floor and
a lower able tarp canopy for a roof.

At Easter time, in 1941, eighteen boys, my brother and I included,
went through Sequoia National forest in California, then up into
Yosemite for all its wonders in such a setup.

Inside our new, much, much better rig with the kids getting eats
from the fridge, jumping on the beds and fighting for the co-pilot's seat.

A loud bang while we were on I-15, climbing out of San Bernardino on the way to Barstow. I pulled off, got out and kicked tires, checked the rig for other yet unknown problems.

Almost immediately after this worrisome event happened, we pulled into the next small remote gas station along the highway. I told the mechanic about the loud bang.

Quickly checking us out, "Yep! The pop-off safety valve let go on the propane tank. Caused by the desert heat. No harm done."

I offered to pay, but the man waved me off with a handshake.

Now, much more relaxed when crossing the dessert, we pulled into a KOA Camp. Our first hook up experience took quite a bit of time and experimenting for all of us.

Most of us helped fixing our first dinner with this totally new experience. That propane stove was an adventure.

Luckily, for me, the bedding choices were without chaos. Kirk and Keith on the two rear over and under beds, Rob on the convertible single bed and Kev and I on the pull down over the driver's space.

So, easily at dawn, after each of us had the breakfast we'd planned for this venture, our team reversed the hookups and stowed all the parts used.

A few more hours' drive and we were now parked in the middle of Hoover Dam where we took the tour down into the working parts of this historical national monument. Quite an eye opener of what we needed to survive.

The Kids at Hoover Dam

Back on the road, Robin, now in the co-pilot's seat, Kev and Keith at the dining table while Kirk stood behind my driver's chair. "Gee, wouldn't it be great if Mom was here?" he said.

Without turning to add his thoughts, "Hey, you guys were there when I asked her. Even offered to wait until she cleared her calendar."

Next stop to investigate was the Petrified Forest just north of the famous Route 66 early into Arizona.

Next is one of the most impressive sights and a major part of my thoughts until this day, was Arizona's Meteor Crater, elevation 5,710 feet. Kirk and Robin hiked to the 560-foot bottom of the three quarters of a mile wide crater while Keith, Kev and I watched from our rig at the edge of this tremendous hole in our planet, created with unbelievable force from the heavens centuries ago. More than likely changing the orbit of our planet?

At the Grand Canyon, of course, we were awed with its centuries of hidden majesty. We all agreed and passed on a two daytrip, by mule, to the bottom of the canyon.

After a few days of wending our way from Arizona up into the Black Hills of South Dakota and the amazing, chiseled hills of Mount Rushmore, we took time to report home to Mom.

Fun scene with me in the outdoor phone booth calling home. Our four were almost out of control pushing each other for the next position. The relief summer babysitter answered since Ruth was off for a month to both visit and attend business in her original home area of Alabama.

"Yea, Jackie, the kids are having a really great time. All the sweat is well worth it. Say, what about you meeting us at Lou and Roger's in a few days and ...? Is ... " a pause, "sure, wait a minute."

I opened the door the rest of the way and, "Rob, Mom wants to talk to you."

The beaming Robin entered the space, took the phone, and struggled to shut the booth door. The three boys are excited in anticipation of their each having their coming turns with Mom. The shot through the booth glass of Robin's enthusiasm as she talks with Jackie is so energetic, it's hard to describe that moment.

On each of the next three calling events the scene was repeated three more times.

When Kevin was finally finished, with a confused look, he hung up the phone and opened the door.

I asked, "What about ...?"

Kev just shrugs with, "Dad, she just said goodbye and told me to hang up."

Musing a moment, I shrugged and came up with, "Okay, then, let's saddle up and get back on the road. Got to get to Custer's Last Stand and then on to Yellowstone."

Obviously excited, Robin jumped in with, "That's where Old Faithful does its thing, isn't it, Dad?"

With a confused smile, "Right on, dear one."

Our rig, now wending from the Black Hills of South Dakota and back onto I-90 traveling west to the Crow Reservation in Montana.

Pulling into that Crow reservation area in the deep dark of night there were rock band sounds as very kind helpers guide our rig into a parking spot with hand-held flashlights. We would never have made it without their help. At midnight the rock sounds stopped, and the traditional Crow ceremonial drums took over until dawn.

As the sun raised us and we did our morning Beechwood chores, we prepared to check out the area of Memorial Hill. This area has had so much written history about it: Custer's Last Stand. It was eight minutes east of us here.

It was just within a half hour of sunrise when we pulled up to the blocked off area which contains the graves of Custer's troops. ...All of us get out and check out the small area where Custer's troops lie buried.

I come out with, "Think this over guys. Down there on that river were over six thousand of the finest fighters of the Sioux Nation and that idiot Custer took them on with two hundred and seventy-six men. That's what an out-of-control ego will do to you."

The varying reaction of each child took some minutes to reflect on my thoughts.

Then, we moved on down the ridge to where Major Reno's historic stand took place. Once more we looked down at The Little Big Horn River, far below, where more than six thousand Teton Sioux warriors had been camped.

That heroic Major Reno place on that hill is now referred to as "Medal of Honor Hill". Snapping the thoughts from them at this once-in-a-life-time moment, "Okay kids, let's saddle up and on to Yellowstone by tomorrow.

The almost 250 miles to Yellowstone from the reservation took a bit over five hours. Some travel time was enthusiastically used stopping to take in the amazing scenes of nature rarely seen en route, unless lucky, as we are on this trip.

Entering the north entrance of Yellowstone Park and making our way south to the area of the most famous tourist attractions.

The kids were in awe of the breathtaking scenery. Kevin even enjoyed a Popsicle from our small freezer.

Old Faithful did its business while an ill Robin watched the event from the back bed while the boys and I were able to move as close as publicly allowed.

The greatest spots were covered within hours; we found the commercial area where we reload supplies for the rig in West Thumb.

After refueling our 120-gallon fuel tank, using 8 gallons a mile, I re-started the engine with, "Okay, gang, gotta lot of miles to make it to Lou and Roger's. At least two days ... I hope ... unless some creeks arise."

The just under 1200 miles to Santa Rosa and Roger and Lou's went without problems. The 'You are Now Entering California' sign at the Nevada border created whoops and hollers from the troops on board.

Up highway 101, the Santa Rosa sign created screams and yells.

Driving up the in-road up to Lou and Roger's two plus acre very rural hilltop home gave me great relief. I could rest. No driving for a few days. Their lovely pool? Relaxing in the sun for a change.

My four having a ball with Andy and Nancy in and out of the pool and wherever kids can find to discover new ideas and projects.

I called home to find out that Stu Philips has a film scoring session he wants me on within a week.

While loading to leave, Roger, once again surveying our rig, "Sure a lovely way to travel, Dave."

With hearty laughs, "Can you imagine the five of us in my truck? Ya gotta remember our Easter trip with Mister Wilding?"

After a swig from his beer can, "Much bigger truck than your Dodge." Lou, joining in, "Too bad Jackie had to miss it all. This is her sort of trip."

The long drive from 101 and merging over to I-5 at the east of the Bay Area, took just under nine hours. I pull the Beechwood up in the north 144 Van Ness drive. Our Pontiac wagon's pad in front was empty.

The rig door burst open just as we came to a stop. All four kids race, jump out the door and bolt up the lawn and over the empty parking pad to cram through the front door with screams of "Mom. Mom, we're home. Mom?"

Since our eight-year live-in nanny, child beater RUTH had been given the summer off, a young temp babysitter came out from the family room.

She started with, "Hi, guys. Your Mom's at work. She's due home in time for dinner ... a little after five."

Our disappointed group shrugged her words off and started enjoying just being home. Kirk went out the back slider, kicked off his shoes, dropped his shirt, and dove into the pool.

K2 and K3 followed close behind while Robin started upstairs to her room. I entered, carrying a duffel bag.

She greeted me with, "Hi, Mister Ward. So, how'd it go?"

"Fine ... really fine. Tiring, but fine. Being the only driver took a lot of my day. Very, very glad to be home. I'm sure the Home Wreckers are, too."

She giggled with, "Mrs. Ward's at work. Seems like a last-minute call to do a commercial that she couldn't turn down. Someone named Al Alan."

I grumbled, "Al has a problem with his last-minute gigs. He has trouble getting the agency people trained to work the right way. Oh, well, what ...."

"She said she'd be home a bit after five."

I checked my watch. "Another real quickie, I guess."

Within ten minutes, our gray-green family Pontiac station wagon pulled in, off Van Ness and onto the parking pad we'd created on the front lawn area. Jackie, obviously seeing the Beechwood, jumped out of the wagon with her attaché case, and ran to it and opened the front door.

At that moment, Robin was just coming down the stairs. Jackie quickly dropped her case on the ground as they rushed to each other and grasp.

As they hugged and kissed, "Hey, Mom. Wow! How great it ...."

The boys, hearing Robin's greetings, scrambled to this scene from the family room. The hugging and kissing went on for quite a while.

I slowly came into the hallway to see this great moment. Jackie looked up, smiled while still holding all four children.

"Hi. How'd it go? Any troubles?"

Continuing to relish this scene for many moments, "Oh, fine. Much, much better than it could have ever been in the flat bed abortion".

Standing and slowly taking each child in, "Did they cause any ...?"

"Really great. They were all so great. They grew up one hell of a lot during those days on the road. You would have been so proud. They were just so great. Each one had a couple of kinda bad days, but with the motor home whoever was not feeling well just stayed in bed while we were able to keep rolling on. Kirk saw the Mesa Verde cliff dwellings from the rear bed window. Didn't get to go down inside, but at least saw them. Robin had the same deal in Yellowstone. From the back window Old Faithful did its thing."

She singled out Keith and Kevin, patting each, "What about these two?" "A few sniffles, but nothing slowed them down."

Both swell up a bit with my almost compliment.

As the group moved into the family room, the babysitter asked, "Missus Ward, what would you like for dinner?"

She looked down at each while considering her answer. "Any objections to going to Carnation?"

No surprise with their reactions of whoops and hollers: "Yeah," "Let's go," etc. They start to bolt for front door.

"Whoa, slow down," she cautioned, "give me a couple of minutes to check with Nina." She went to the wall phone above the kitchen dining counter.

Our almost favorite family place for the best meals was at 5045 Wilshire Blvd, just one block west of Highland Avenue, on the north side of the boulevard ... just at the eastern edge of the Miracle Mile. The six of us, plus the babysitter were seated. Kevin's having a very private whispering conversation with Mom as she reacts, highly animated.

Kirk and Keith join him as Kevin jabbed Keith for interrupting his time.

Jackie admonished them all with, "Hey, guys, we're home and we have plenty of time to hear all your great stories."

Robin threw in, "... and Dad has a lot of film, too."

Looking at me, with a smile, "Maybe we can see them Sunday after Dad gets them developed."

I added, "I'll turn it in after we get home. Checking in with Jimmie, we have a session on Monday, so I have to get back at it."

The excited monsters settle into their seats when the two waitresses bring the food.

It's Sunday, so the babysitter has the day off. My 8mm projector is running films of the trip. I was at my desk working in the den on Jimmie's pages, with the swinging door blocked open so I could watch the films of the trip in the family room. It's quite a scene with all the reactions of the kids trying to explain to Mom what each event was to each of them.

Robin whooped a bit with, "See! Ya see? Kirk and I ran all the way to the bottom of that famous huge crater."

The tape reel ended so I got up to load the next three-minute reel. Jackie sat on the couch with all four children packed in against her.

When I finished the re-loading, I turned to them, "I think this is when we were at the Little Big Horn."

Keith moved to face Jackie to tell her, "Hey, Mom, that's where a general named Custer fought almost seven thousand Sioux Indians with only two hundred and fifty troops."

Shaking his head Kirk corrected Keith's statement with a snide, "Two hundred and seventy-six, stupid."

As Keith withdrew a bit, Jackie took Kirk's arm with a slight squeeze, "Come on now, Kirk." She turned back to Keith. "That was very interesting, Keith. So good you were so close. Thank you."

Robin now had her two cents to add, leaning toward Jackie, "Dad told us that was on your birthday, Mom."

With a look of total surprise, "June twenty-fifth?"

Kev threw in his two cents with, "Yep, June twenty-fifth." With a look and a giggle, "A few years earlier, though."

As I finished the re-load and started the projector again, "really?" The kids all broke up while Jackie just shrugs the comment off.

THE SOUPY SESSION

A few nights later, about 01:10 AM, I'm working when a lite rap on the front door happened. I put my pen in its holder and made my way to meet the expected messenger. I opened the door, and the messenger handed me a package.

Very quietly I said, "Thanks." I started to turn but back at the messenger with, "thanks for the knuckles lightly on the door rather than the doorbell. Don't want to take a chance on waking anyone."

He replied with a huge smile and a 'thumbs up.' "See you in a couple of hours, I guess."

As I slowly closed the door, "I hope it's only a couple of hours. I'd like to get at least an hour's sleep before the session."

We were setting up the Soupy Sales session in Studio "A" at Capitol Records as I passed out the parts to each musician's stand while Jimmie's talking with Soupy at his podium.

"This should be a lot of fun today. I'm such a big fan of your show."

Frank Nastasi, who played the characters White Fang and Black Tooth, is having fun with about six nine- to twelve-year-olds in a corner of the studio. Kirk's one of them, having been invited by Jimmie.

Patting Jim's arm, "I'm looking forward to it. It was so much fun getting the material ready. Kinda new thing for us."

Having finished the setup, I moved to the podium and waited for Jim to recognize me. Interrupting this dialogue, Jim reached out to me and, "Oh, Soupy, I'd like you to meet the fellow who makes sense out of all my hen scratching and mistakes, David Ward."

Soupy offers his hand. Shaking hands, "So very pleased to meet you. I've always admired the pressure and work that copyists have to go through."

As I blushed and squeezed his grip at tad more. "Were you able to get any sleep," Jim asks.

"I will when I get home."

Taking a step back while surveying me, "You mean you've been up all ...."

With a slight blush and grin at Jim, "It happens a lot with Jimmie's hectic schedule."

Patting my shoulder, "Dave is the last one on the totem pole. He doesn't make it, we don't make it. He's never failed.

Soupy extends his hand again with an additional pat on my hand, "Sounds like when I work on a deadline."

During a ten, while listening to play backs, Black Fang continued frolicking with the guest children.

The session is just now over, as the musicians are packing up, while more pictures are being taken. Soupy wants one with Kirk. As hard as Soupy tries, Kirk won't smile. The whole production crew is in hysterics because Soupy can't get Kirk to do anything but frown while looking up at him.

I got to a photographer. "Any chance to get a copy of that?" Shaking with laughter, the camera man gives me a 'thumbs up.'

THE BEGINNING
OF THE END

In mid-August of 1969, I was working on a Stu Phillips score for a film recording session of *The Curious Female*.

Back and forth from Stu's new Studio City home in the Valley, I was able to use our wagon rather than the camper ... when Jackie wasn't using it.

I was picking up another arrangement from Stu's studio, in Studio City, just off Laurel Canyon, from beside his newly crafted pool. The pool he forced Anthony Pools to put in in ten days after hearing that Sinatra had his pool put in and filled within seven days.

(NOTE: That pool has since been moved to a better area between the main house buildings and a tennis court now sits on that same space, high and dry.)

I worked late into the early morning of Sunday, the 17th. Stu's session wasn't until Tuesday, but I wanted to finish tomorrow so I could get to Big Bear to lay out my newest scheme for the leftover food on the Anderson's Smorgasbord tables.

I gave up about 03:25 with only three short cues left to do. Quietly into the house and slipped into bed at 03:35. Jackie was fast asleep.

My alarm went off at 06:20 causing Jackie to just roll over but stay asleep.

I worked all day in the studio with my summer vacation children dropping in and out all day with their problems while swimming in the pool.

I was only able to get two of the three cues done before I had to get some sleep. The orchestra was halfway big. Eight brass, five reeds, twenty-two strings and six rhythm.

Back down from my cave and sneaked quietly into bed at 04:30.

I struggled awake and sat up in bed at 08:45, scratched and rubbed my head. I swung my feet toward the floor and paused. Jackie was just finishing dressing in the closet about six feet away from me.

As I continued scratching while speaking to somewhere in the room, "Oh hell, thank Her that at least I'm down to the last cue on this mess."

(NOTE: Our live-in housekeeper, Ruth - our children's warden for the past eight years -had been given this month off to attend family business in Alabama. We now have a young girl replacement on a daily basis).

Jackie started out of the closet but moved back in. She's quiet and not up to the usual humming or warming up her voice.

As I searched for my slippers I asked, "What's your day like?"

No answer.

Here we leave the opening shock scene and enter into the 'how life must go on' part of this family tragedy.

ROGERS'S LIVING ROOM, SEPTEMBER 20, 1969

Lou had just finished up in her kitchen while Roger slouched in his favorite armchair with a beer in hand. I sat slouched on the couch watching some uninteresting football game on the tube.

Lou came in from the kitchen with a cup of something which she set on the other end of my couch spot.

With a very frustrated voice, "Damnit to hell, what I can't understand is when you two guys were here in June, Jackie told me, "If anything ever happened to David, I couldn't live. I just couldn't take it." What happened to her in these past three months?" After a sip from his can, very slowly, "Alyce Lou, we have no idea what could have happened to ...."

She threw her hands up, "But, in just three months? She said that your trip to Europe was the best time she'd had since you were married. And, and even Janice is blown away. She has no clue either".

I looked over to check out Lou's frustration. "I had no idea. Did she say that?"

She, in a heated flash, pounding on the cushion between us, turned her rage toward me with, "While you and Roger were out in the yard.

That's when she told me that. I just can't figure. I thought I knew her so well."

Crunching his now empty can, "Lou, Lou, Lou there's no way of knowing."

Jerking around to face Roger, "Do you think I should call her? Maybe she'd ... maybe call Beatta?

Roger, as he rose, threw the crunched can in the waste basket with, "Stay out of it. She's your best friend and ...."

Lou blasts, "I just want to help. Four wonderful kids. I just can't figure ... What if I called Beatta?"

I heard the fridge door open, and Rog fumbled another beer out of its pack and drops it to the floor which he picks up with, "Shit."

As she continued her frustration and rage, she turned to me and reached out to touch my arm.

With a concerned and compassionate look, "Has she ever done strange things like that?"

After what must have seemed hours of reflection on that question, I readjusted my seating position a bit.

Clearing my throat, "Well," a moment, "when Robin was just about a year old, a Jehovah's witness, Gretchen, got a hold of her. She was at our house for a couple of hours most days ... 'specially when I was not working at home, but at Cameo."

Leaning back gathering in what she knew about The Witnesses, "What a total pain in the ass when they get their foot through the door."

With a slight reflecting smile, "Gretchen had everything she had through that door. Books, schedules, promises, everything. I'd learned to avoid those sessions when I got home."

I rose and paced, "After a couple of weeks of all this she announced that she'd like us to consider selling the house, taking Robin and moving into whatever the Witness had to offer. Join them entirely."

Walking over to the slider and looking out into their garden, I talked to the glass while Lou sat where she was. With a slow grin at the glass, I turned to face her with, "Having learned how Jackie with her 'instant answer' history, I thought the situation out very carefully. I think it might have been the next day ... or could've been two days... who knows now, I told her that if she really felt the calling she was free to leave Robin with me and go on to her new calling. I guess the quiet, calm, stern way I laid it out, that was the end of Gretchen for us."

I just had to get the hell out of their house. Lou's frustrating questions were just piling more turds higher on my un-flushable heap.

Why? No idea why/how but, before driving the torturous route south, I, for a last time, took the Beech down the Russian river, passed my Ward Ranch gate, on State Route 116, past our favorite family Ryan's Beach, through Duncan's Mills on to where the Russian finished her long California trip back to the Pacific Ocean.

That night, I parked on the sand, staring out my window at the waves slashing on the shore was extremely beneficial in calming me in my short time in my sleeping bag.

Just after dawn, I drove the very short distance south to Bodega Bay where I walked the levee where the movie, *The Birds* was filmed. Almost funny how similar chaos had now invaded my life. I Pray for a good ending to this true-life story with so much at stake.

Reflecting back once again, during this thirty-one-day period I slept less than two hours a night and ate nor drank nothing. Lost a bit over fifty-five pounds from a bulging 240 gut pounds down to a normal one-eighty-five and a much shorter belt size.

So many ... so many ... too many people have told me it couldn't have been done. "Ya just gotta have water?"

"Fuck 'em!"

It's so interesting, that since I believed I'm one of the most unrecognized religious people alive that I could truly understand how some fathers could kill their entire family? No religious nor legal consequences were ever of concern to me while I drove back and forth in my personal tragic hell. To lose my family within a few months for a never known nor explained reason? From heaven to the gates and fires of hell in just a few days and never learn why.

What more hell could there be for me? It took meeting up with attorney Loyd Saunders that made that thought slowly fade away.

A few weeks later yet another long drive up the I-5, to merge over the Bay Bridges and onto the 101 and into Santa Rosa, to emotionally cry to Roger and Lou since they've been so involved with my history with my life with Jackie.

SEPTEMBER 25, 1969

My Mother happened to be there with Lou and Roger while I, once again, slouched on the family room couch. Mother suggested to the group, "What about the idea of going out to dinner tonight? I think it would be a fine idea."

Lou perks up with, "Yes. Sure, Mark West would be just great." I'm not impressed nor motivated, "You three go. I'll stay here and watch the kids."

Mother almost jumped up with, "No. No, you must join us. Just shower and get dressed up just a bit. It will do you a world of good to get out."

Scowling at her, "But, I'm not hungry."

Pressing on, she continued with, "That's fine. Just sit and visit with us. I have to go home tomorrow. It's my last night. Please?"

Very reluctantly I got up and left to perform minimal prep work.

Roger called after me, "Okay if we leave at five-thirty?" With a wave of my hand indicating okay, I continued out toward the shower.

After I'd disappeared, Roger gave a Thumbs Up to the rest in the room as he picked up the phone with, "I'd better make reservations for four. Busy weekend night."

The famous Mark West Northern California eatery is located just less than four miles north of Santa Rosa and just about two hundred yards east of The Redwood Highway 101 on the one and only famous *Peanuts'* Charles Schulz Airport Road.

As we were ushered to our table, after we'd settled in, the maitre'd handed out menus. I waved mine off which was coyly noticed by the others.

Finally seated, the four of us, Mother, opposite Lou with Roger on her left and me on her right, showered and barely presentable with my limited traveling wardrobe in my one suitcase outfit.

A charming tall, young waitress has just collected the three menus from the others.

Mother puts her hand on my arm as she leans toward me, "Won't you please have something?" She looks at the others." Something to just keep us company?"

With huge sighs and highly disgruntled, I condescend with, "Okay, damn it, I'll have a cup of coffee ...," looking up at the striking looking waitress, "later."

Having given in, I sulked back into my chair and glowered at Mother. "Aw, come on, Mother, not like I was eight, please."

Suddenly hyped, I attack her with, "on our way to Reno in 1934, some roadway eatery where you created my overdone coffee with heavy cream," becomes more up, "and in those days it was really cream, and you overloaded the sugar with at least four teaspoons thereby hooking me for life."

I lightly pounded the table with a daring look at her as the creator of the beginning problems in my life.

Flustered, she blurts out with, "You used to like your coffee that way when ...."

With a slow, cold look at her, "I think I've outgrown that time of life. Haven't I?"

When I finished my last drop, I looked into the now empty cup and slowly placed it back on its saucer in very slow motion. Fondling it as it now sits there, empty.

Early the next morning, having survived my traumatic last night dinner outing—under pressure—with very little sleep, I entered the kitchen where Lou is well into getting breakfast started for this new day.

Andy and Nancy are anxiously seated in the dinette area, eagerly waiting for this day's starters.

Mother's daubing her tea bag while sitting across from the two young Wards.

Turning from the range, Lou, seeing me, "Oh, good morning, David. Any rest?" Just a shrug is all from me. "Can I fix you something?"

As I slowly moved thru the room, with a very slow thought, at the doorway, into the den, I stopped, and, back over my shoulder, I add, "Maybe just some coffee." And, after a long beat, "Do you happen to have an English muffin?"

Silent panic as Lou and Mother are in awe. Tears rolled from Mother's eyes.

After abusing my great supportive family once more, during my time of crisis, I pointed my Beech south down its fast becoming my most hated route in this State of my beloved California.

Still at a total geographical loss of the place where I belong, I, for some unknown, unexplainable reason headed to Whittier, and Barry and Sharon's home.

BARRY & SHARON'S, SEPTEMBER 28. 1969

The Beech and I arrived in front of Barry and Sharon's Whittier home just after about 04:38 on a day of the week I can't remember. The dawn is still just about two hours off. The number of those tremendously emotional trips on that new major California highway have become lost in my screwed-up haze memory of so many emotional/panicked trips ... while crying.

So lucky to find the space right in front of their home. Parking was simple just fitting the Beech between the two driveways.

It had to be almost 08:45 when my lovely twenty-six-year-old niece, SALTU, (Sharon Ann Lundigan Trory Uzel) knocked on the Beech front door.

Stumbling out of my tired sleeping bag and making it to the door, I opened to my dear niece, Sharon.

With her great look, she asks, "well, hi, Uncle Bidu, when did you get here?' "Kinda late this morning. Drove down from Lou and Roger's."

She climbs into the rig while I find my pants and pull them on and search under the recesses for my shoes.

Sitting at the table, she continues our conversation with, "I've talked with G.G. and she said you finally started to eat. Golly, you look awful, how much weight have you lost?"

Finding my loafers, pulling one on, "I have no idea."

Standing and moving down one step in the doorway, she reaches for my hand with, "Hey, Come on in. Barry's gone to work." with a huge smile and a squeeze, "Would you like something to eat?"

About 17:50, Sharon's late twenties husband, Barry, comes through the front door and tossing his packages on the sofa, warm handshakes happened.

INFO: They were married in our home to eliminate religious background problems: He's Jewish, she's protestant.

"Great. I saw the motor home in front when I left this morning.

Barry, now comfortably inside, Saltu came from another room, and with hugs and kisses being exchanged between them. Still holding on, she offered, "I would have called you, but I knew you were up to your ears in meetings all day."

A squeeze and, "Yeah, but you could have left a message. I would have picked it up sometime during the day."

Feeling reprimanded, "I'm sorry, honey, I guess I could have."

Letting go of her, he asked me, "Can you spend some time with us? You're welcome to use our guest room."

As she was leaving the scene, hearing this offer, her pleasure needed no further description. As I crossed the room and picked up my jacket from the sofa, a slow silent reply runs through my head, "What the hell, in our accounting firm, that money tiger, Norm Greenbaum split our joint checking account in half. For me, about thirteen hundred to live on. I can't work. My pens are useless. All other monies are frozen up tight. What a hell of a steep uphill future stands in my way."

As I neared the front door, "Thanks for the wonderful offer, you two. I can't make any plans, so this is a great start to keep me off the roads. I'll just go and get a couple of life sustaining things from the Beech.

I made my way down the front steps and entered the rig where, from the cabinet over the sink and drawer below, I put a few essentials into a small overnight bag.

Checking the wardrobe closet, I passed what it had to offer for this moment, grabbed the essentials bag and went out the door and back up the steps and into the warm, loving, helpful Uzel house ... my current lifesavers.

Barry had gone to retrieve a second beer from the fridge and just came through that doorway as I re-entered from the front porch. Closing the door, I moved off to the small guest bedroom where I dumped my bag on the bed and returned to where he had just switched on the TV for the six o'clock news on NBC. Seeing me back, he muted the audio.

Flopping into a second lounger, usually Sharon's, I dumped more turds with, "Shit, I have no plans. Just going from hour to hour and day to day. Even thinking ... saw an ad for a free flight lesson at Fullerton Airport."

From the kitchen, overhearing this thought, she came to the door opening and scanned Barry with a fright look.

Taking a swig, "Who knows? Might be real fun." a second sip and, "Well, take your time. Get it all together ... safely all together."

While touching all my fingers to each other, "Thanks, Barry. I so gratefully appreciate your help and offer. Lou is totally shocked and poor Roger's hard at work to back her off. She wants to call everybody, Jackie, Beatta, Janice."

Looking to see Sharon leaning against the door jamb, "Your Mother suggested that I get in touch with Bertha Saunders' son, Loyd... To protect your interests.

I laughed, "Protect what? This is California. What in hell does a man have in divorce court? The song *Born to Lose* really fits fathers." I slammed my fist on the chairs arm with, "Is there an answer? Is there a reason that I can't find an answer?"

OCTOBER 1, 1969,
LOSING ALL MY ASSETS

Somehow ... where and how I don't remember, I received a legal notice to appear at Jackie's attorney's offices, Stern, Blakely and Kahn, out next to LAX, on a certain specified day.

When there, almost totally unrecognizable, due to weight loss and scabs, I was forced to sign over our Big Bear store back to the Cravens, who were there for this turnover. Next, the 322-acre Ward Ranch documents back to my Dad, our Big Bear home and three lots, in Bear City, all back to their respective banks.

That scene was ever so legal and cold.

Some uncountable days later I had my first moments with Paul, Dr. Paul Reichlie, who was a major player in building my/our wonderful family.

Having been told by Office Ruler Grace, near the front desk that his last patient of the day had just left, I made my way into his office. A frozen moment of recognition when he threw his letter opening tool on the desk and turned away from me.

Seconds passed as he slowly turned his swivel back to face me. I moved closer and flopped in a desk chair. Long silent looks as he picked up that letter opener and jabbed it into the blotter protecting his desk.

Almost fuming, "Okay! Okay! What, in all hell, is all this shit I hear? Is she nuts?"

"You've heard right. She's flipped. She won't talk to anyone but her lawyer. Even Janice, her sister I wouldn't talk to for two years, says she has no idea what her thinking is."

Another 360 rotation on that chair and, "She has a real problem. In all my years in practice and delivering babies, she's the favorite of all my ladies. I thought she had her feet so well planted and has such a great, really one of the finest I've ever delivered, family."

I leaned in a bit with, "I hear she's going to some other doctor and ...."

He leaned back and looked to the ceiling and coming back to face me with a vicious look, again pounding his fist on the desk, "That sure fits the pattern" a slight laugh, "I'm not sure what pattern. Hell, I need a drink." looking at me, "nuts, you don't drink."

"Not in one of a hell of a long time."

Looking at his newly marked desk blotter, "It fits the pattern. She doesn't want to face me to hear what bawling out I'd have to say."

"That's too bad. She adores you and your opinion and all the great times we've had having our four kids with your help." Some reflective moments until I broke the silence with, "You remember about my breaking my thirty-one day fast with a cup of coffee?"

A sharp look at me and he nodded.

Fingering my gold treble clef hanging around my neck, "When I got back south, my body broke out with the biggest sores all over." With a knowing look, "Bet in your hair, too?"

Laughing, and shaking my head, "Oh, hell yes. Jackie's sister, Janice, insisted that I go see a dermatologist and even drove me to hers. I was mending by then, so just some salve to speed up the natural healing process."

Paul rose from his desk and moved around the corner. He sternly addressed me with, "You know, David, that's your home just as much as it is hers. If I were you, I'd move back in and suggest that she, and her mother, can leave if they can't handle it. God, I think I'll get drunk tonight. I have no ladies close to term." with a look, "Wanna join me? You can't afford the tab now with her legal team castrating you."

Just a blank stare.

For some strange reason, the thought I threw out in Barry and Sharon's living room those days ago, re-appeared with me at the Fullerton Municipal Airport with me, sitting, with an instructor, in a single engine Piper Cub at the head of the takeoff runway ... seat belts secured.

After getting airborne, for this approximately thirty-minute demo ride, the instructor explained the very few, simple dash of instruments.

When he handed me the flight stick and I made such simple maneuvers carefully, very carefully with his instructions, my mind drifted to, "What the hell, what more can I lose? I took a complimentary flight to see what more threatening things might happen in my life. Even considered taking up smoking and drinking again."

GINNY SUGGESTS LOYD

Back on ground, in my mother's living room with unknown or explained pressures building by the moment, sitting in an overstuffed living room chair. My older sister, Ginny, sat on the couch holding a cup of tea.

My birth was on July 8, 1927. Hers: July 9ᵗʰ 1924. She had been told that I was her birthday present. That present lasted for our lifetime ... through all our horrible youth and life's horrible trials. Hers, much more than mine.

Mother stayed in the kitchen/den area, out of the way while we exchanged our great disappointments. This, being currant and most urgent, she asks, "Do you have any idea of what you're going to do when January first comes?"

With actions showing frustration, "January first?"

Stroking her teacup, "That's when the new divorce law comes into effect. The new, no-fault law. No reason necessary. No charges. No making up phony excuses. No lying needed anymore."

Quiet moments with head shaking and tossing, "So, what do I have to ...?"

Putting her cup on the low table in front of her, "I would think you need to have a lawyer to protect your ...."

More frustrated squirming and, "Well, she's got it licked. What would I fight with? A man hasn't got a chance in California. The divorce history's ...."

Calmly shaking her head, "Well, I'll tell you one thing, I'd sure as hell make her tell the court what she's up to. Put it on the record. Make her face you there and tell it to your face. Don't just let her and her attorneys push the divorce through without at least a couple of answers going on the record."

Looking to my lap and then facing her, "Attorney? Why do I need an attorney? I don't know an attorney. I've heard the ones she has are top pros. I guess John Baylor put her onto them."

"John Baylor? Who's he?"

"A sick group singer she works with all the time. A real loser. A screwed up egotistical mess."

With a stern look at me, "I'd still make them tell you, to your face, what this is all about. Don't let them make up their version and lie to make you look bad in court."

Fidgeting, "I don't have any ...." I rose, crossed the room, and peered out the window. With a slight nod Ginny asked, "Do you remember Loyd Saunders?"

Trying to get my brain to recall that name, "Loyd? You mean Bertha's son?" With a look of accomplishment, "Yes, Loyd, Bertha's son."

"So what? So, I haven't seen him in ... maybe twenty years. Not since I was in Fairfax." Now, very calmly, she introduced me with, "Loyd is one of the best divorce attorneys in California. Actually, west of the Mississippi."

I turned to face her with an intensely interested look, "Really? You mean Bertha's son? Mother's great friend, old Bertha's son?"

As she lit up a new cigarette, "I went out with Loyd for a short time when Jack and I were getting our divorce. I'd give him a call. What can it hurt?"

She got up, went into the den where she found the white pages, looked up a number, penciled a note, tore it off the pad and returned.

She handed it to me with, "Here. Here's his number. Give it a try. What can it hurt? At least find out what your options are. You've got four great kids to protect, if nothing else. At least find out."

With all the legal confusion, being forced, by Jackie's attorneys to return all the properties I'd gathered during our married years, Barry had come up with a startling discovery: an attorney, connected with his bank, a real estate attorney in Beverly Hills, at Barry's request checked out our deal with buying the Craven Hardware store. Great for its original plan, a disaster when it closed, and it was then converted into Anderson's Smorgasbord.

Asked to meet with this fellow, at his office, just up Beverly Drive a few hundred yards north of Wilshire Blvd, the meet was short and horribly sweet.

This extremely well-prepared Youngman, facing me from across his desk, shattered me with, "Really strange, David. We found out that Craven sold you the business he'd just closed the street. In no way what he sold you was the business you bought and suffered such a loss with."

OCTOBER 9, 1969

At long last, after many, many pushes from others, I made it to the One Wilshire Building to re-meet Bertha's son, attorney Loyd Saunders, partner with Saul Ross.

As the elevator door opened and I exited, I checked names on office doors.

At the Ross and Saunders door, I stopped and checked my paper notes, then I opened the door.

Slowly entering, a mid-thirties attractive Teri sat at the front desk with a few years older, totally efficient looking Ester, with her desk further back in an alcove.

Rising and extending her hand, Teri says, "Hi! I could guess that you're David. David Ward, right?"

"Yeah. Uh huh."

"Good. I need to get some details from you. Mister Saunders will be with you shortly after. Did you park in the building?"

Slowly adjusting, "No. All I have for wheels is my twenty-eight-foot Beechwood motor home and my Honda 90 Trail Bike. Jackie has the wagon, so I drove the Beechwood downtown. It's very hard to find a place to park something that big close, so I finally found a spot over on Figueroa and walked here."

Teri looked back towards Esther.

"That's quite a walk. Over eight blocks."

Almost grinning, "I've got nothing but time these days." She then motioned me to the chair in front of her desk where the necessary interrogation process began.

A manila folder as well as her computer screen become filed with necessary data.

After this forty-plus minutes of data collecting, when she'd finished, Esther rose and moved to greet me.

Extending her hand, "Hi, David, I'm Ester. Wish I could say nice to meet you. Please follow me."

I rose, with a thanks gesture back at Teri, I followed her into Loyd's office."

Loyd Saunders is a quite tall man, approx. 6'3", who has a remarkable resemblance to famous Scandinavian actor, Max Van Syndow. He was wearing light tan slacks; a complementary sports coat draped over the back of his chair. Wide suspenders keep his slacks where he wants them. He took a large cigar from his mouth and offered his hand.

"David, it's been a long, long time."

After shaking hands, "It has been, but I really don't ... how's your mother?"

Putting his cigar in the large desk ashtray, "Mom is just fine. Don't know if you've heard, but she and Terry sold their place on Lexington and have moved to Joshua Tree about two years ago. The high desert seems to agree with them much better."

He gestured, "Have a seat. Let's see what we can do for you." He re-lit the shortened stub of his cigar, leaned back, blowing smoke toward the ceiling, then leaned forward to me with a serious look. "Do you want this divorce?"

Confused with his direct attack, "Oh, hell no! Hell no!" Leaning back a bit, "Are you in a hurry to get this matter over with?"

That question attacked my thinking to the point where I must recover the shock of his demanding question.

My stern look seemed to give him his answer.

Fumbling through Teri's notes in front of him, he puffed and looked out his 10th floor window at downtown Los Angeles below.

Returning to face me, again fumbling Teri's notes, "Well, it seems you wife has engaged the law firm of Khan, Stern and Blaney, right?"

"That's what I've been told. That's what the papers said."

Again, looking out the window and spinning back at me with, "Well, that's mistake number one."

I'm now totally confused. Mistake number one. What in hell does that mean? I perk up and lean a bit forward to learn more. Noticing my sudden interest, "Don't get too excited, please. I only mean that their offices are out by the airport and your home is at one forty-four North Van Ness, correct?"

Relaxing back a bit, I nodded 'yes.'

Another puff and, "... and you say she wants to be in and out of court in one day the first week of January, right?"

"She said that her attorneys told her that the new law would be in effect and there would no longer be any need for grounds. No fault, she said."

Slowly shaking his head several times, "David, there's no way of knowing how things will go after January first of next year and any attorney who thinks he knows, is just nuts."

Stammered, "But I thought ....

Severely pounding his fist on the desk with a seeming attack attitude at me, "Are you an attorney? Or psychic?"

Shocked with that question, "No ... I'm just a music copyist."

Leaning back with yet another puff, "Okay, then you copy music and leave the law to me."

Moving to his page buttons, he pushed one. Esther entered with notebook in hand. Posing an official presence, "Yes?"

Again, out the huge window, without turning, "Esther, would you please tell me, with all your many years of expert knowledge" she stifled a grin, "Approximately how long it takes to get a change of venue through today's courts?"

Thinking where this might be going, "These days?" Facing away

Loyd glares smugly, she answered with, "Anywhere from three to five months.

Loyd slowly rotates his chair to check the slow grin forming on my face.

Now, back in charge of this scene, "That could be well after January one, right?"

All she could do to play her role was nod yes.

With General in command attitude, Loyd demands, "Would you then please draw up the necessary papers for such a change of venue?

Coyly bowing, she grabs the door handle with, "Right away sir," and leaves, closing the door behind her.

Getting a new cigar from its drawer and slowly lighting it, he now glared at me, with the look of a warrior, so hard to explain, "That was their mistake number one."

OCTOBER 28, 1969,
MEET WITH DAD AT
THE MARINA

I'd made arrangements with my father, Estolv Ward to have lunch with me at Marina Del Rey on a bright warm late October day. We sat outside in a semi-private area at a table with a huge umbrella shading our table.

As I looked out over the moored yachts, I said," such a long time since I suffered here."

Dad had a look of questions.

"I was semi-forced to buy the Teri-L because Jackie's dear buddy, Carole Lombard, said that Jackie needed the diversion ... the different relaxation from Big Bear. What a hell of an adventure that mess was. Thirty-two feet of floating hell."

A long, slow look at Dad.

Slapping the tabletop, I lamented, "So sorry I had to put Angela off at this lunch. She has so many ideas and I just want to talk with you. Get your thoughts."

With his looking off, "I understand. I just hope she does. She's so upset with this mess." Getting right to the point, I asked, "When you and Mom went through this crap in 1934, how did you handle it?"

Shaking his head as he sips his coffee, "Got drunk for the first eight months. In those days a divorce took a minimum of a year."

"Jackie's lawyer says, 'one day now.'"

Putting his cup down while cuddling it, "Even though my father was a brilliant lawyer and on my case to fight back, I kept saying, 'but she's the daughter of the Chief Justice of the California Supreme Court. What kind of chance in hell would I have?'"

That reply caused a long pause while Dad reflected at his hurts.

I, very slowly said, "Ironic, isn't it? She wanted to be in show business in Hollywood. A singer in movies."

As he turned away to avoid my face, "It was way too late when I finally showed up. Putting you three on that train to L.A., from the Berkeley station, was the worst moment of my life."

NOVEMBER 12, 1969,
AL PAONESSA
CHRISTMAS PARTY

As I entered his office, Loyd's on the phone. He motioned to me to my usual seat in front of his large, neatly cluttered desk.

When he hung up the phone, with a questioning tone, "Ester says you have an urgent question for me?"

"Yeah, yeah. Yeah. You know my mother?" He slowly nods "yes."

Clearing my throat, "Well, she was talking to her father's old friend, Judge Al Paonessa and he told her that if the minor children don't want the divorce the court would probably disallow it."

With a very long, slow look making me extremely nervous, He looked at the ceiling for what seemed an hour or more.

Finally breaking the silence he asked the ceiling, "Who's your attorney?"

Considering my answer, I slowly said, "Well, you are." Turning to face me, "Then, who are you paying for advice?" Stuttering, "Well, you are."

With his elbows on his desk, he leaned even further toward me with,

"Listening to and taking advice from other people will get you in one whole lot of trouble," stressing, 'one hell of a lot of trouble.' Defensively, "But he's a judge. Retired, but a judge. A retired judge."

Leaning back into his chair, he reached for and lights a cigar stub from his ashtray.

"I know who Al Paonessa is. Superior Court and all that. Not Domestic Court."

Feeling totally defeated by losing my great information, I slumped even more.

Puffing to make sure his lighting up effort worked, "Nobody ... and I mean nobody—that includes this office and me—have any idea of how the courts are going to act when the new law goes into action next January one. I'm sure Jackie's lawyers have told her how easy it'll be without having to make up lies to prove cause as it is now. As of now she has no cause and Paonessa would be quite right." a stern look. "You got that?"

He rises, rounds the desk corner, and leans back on it. "New rules. Don't buy wheels, they'll just claim them as an asset and take them away from you. For now, the motor home and your trail bike they can't touch. Nothing new. Tough, but this game's going to get much tougher."

As his stern words sank in, I came up with a piece of information for him to know.

"Our, now her, accountant, Greenbaum, refused to pay my Diner's Club card bill of $23. My credit is now dead ... useless. Can't buy anything anyway."

During the next two weeks there were three trips to Loyd's office to answer Ester's call for much document signing. I'd gotten a bit smarter by parking the rig in a really out of the way spot and riding my bike so I could park in the One Wilshire parking lot. Put her back on the front rack and back to Sharon and Barry's home in Whittier.

On one trip alone an interrogatory had over three hundred questions to struggle through. Took almost two hours for that trip.

Thanksgiving holiday is usually a great time for family gatherings. It can also be an extremely depressing time for some. For me it was the first major family event where all I could do was get lost by myself.

Once again, I struggled getting the Beechwood up I-5, avoiding Roger and Lou's Santa Rosa home and family. I made it over into the Clear Lake area where I dined on that twenty-seventh day of November at the almost empty Clear Lake Smorgasbord. The usual festive turkey cutouts did very little to make the experience any nicer. Now that I was able to eat again, I filled my plate and sat next to a quite large turkey which I patted when I sat down.

Later I was told by close friends that on December 13, there had been a lavish party at 144 N. Van Ness. The back yard area covered with a tent. A pre-Christmas party went on. I'm sure it must have been thought of by our accountants as a tax write-off. My friend, Tom Kenny asked Jackie, hey Jackie, where's David?"

"Oh, we're getting a divorce."

Stopped dead, Tom talked to several others, gathered his wife and several guests left.

CHRISTMAS DAY, 1969

Yet another great holiday to spend alone. Here at Whittier Narrows Golf Course, there are only a few cars in the parking lot.

"I parked my rig right next to an empty live-in cab of a semi-tractor and played the eighteen holes alone. Did see one twosome and, on anther green, a single man.

JANUARY 2, 1970

How it happened I'm not sure, but, for the first time I was allowed to take my four kids for the weekend. The legal restrictions I was under must have played a heavy part in this slow start of my being with them alone.

I picked Robin, Kirk, Keith and Kevin up on Friday, before dinner time so we could have one of our favorite meals at McDonald's together.

We spent the night in the rig in front of Barry and Sharon's home in Whittier after a quick visit with my mother.

On Saturday it was the first time the rest of my family got to have the day with us. On Sunday, we did the miniature golf thing out near the Whittier Narrows Golf Course. We played the course twice; it was so much fun for all of us.

After dinner at our old family Sunday dinner hangout at Carnation restaurant/fountain on Wilshire Boulevard, it was time to deliver them home.

Pulling up in front of 144 things started getting quite emotional. Seems Beatta was watching for our arrival since the house front door opened before I could open the rig's door. She stood there with the hall light behind her silhouetting her frame. Our station wagon was not on the parking pad.

The kisses and goodbyes seemed to never quit, but I had to push them out and shut the door as they ran crying into the house. It was hard to drive away with the tears blinding me.

Back at Barry and Sharon's, Barry just came home from errands so poor Sharon got most of my horror story of the weekend dumped on her.

"Dear lady ... oh my God, dear lady ... gotta survive a day like today. The kids are so fucked up ... oops, sorry."

"No worry. I've known those words and their frustrations for most of my life." I gave her a big hug. "Just can't take all four when I feel their family life loss the few times, we've tried being together."

"You'll come up with something. There's gotta be a way it'll work."

"I've gotta. Just gotta." A long consoling hug with a kiss on her cheek.

Barry, re-entering the room, "Hey, David, very interesting info. Our bank has records of every law office in the Western United States. We rate all law offices in case we have dealings with them. They rate the attorney's as well as the entire office."

With a look of surprise, "I didn't know that" Sharon threw out.

Smiling back at her, he continued with, "Jackie's Attorneys, Khan, Stern and Blakley are rated so-so. Their office is also so-so. Ross and Saunders are rated the best in the entire Western States. Their office is rated the same. It doesn't seem Ginny gave you bad advice."

Sharon reached and touched my arm. "And you really like him, don't you."

The next day I was driving up Highland Avenue, toward the valley, when I passed the Hollywood Bowl across the road on my left. Totally consumed with this urgent problem, my thoughts were running wildly around my brain.

The only way I can handle this mess is to take them one at a time ... Robin first. The oldest. Her choice of where ... anything she wants to do ... where she might want to go." I slammed the steering wheel. "That's it. One at a time. Each one gets to choose what their weekend will be."

A moment of thought until I reached the Universal off ramp. "Oh shit! What will her lawyers say? Right now, I can't leave the city, the county, or the state without the Courts permission by myself. What if the kids want to go ...? (Gotta write a new screenplay. Maybe call this one 'Their Weekend with Dad'?)

For some, as yet never explained reason, Jackie had taken Robin out of her John Burroughs Junior High and Kirk out of Van Ness School and put them into a small one room schoolroom on La Brea Avenue, next to the La Brea movie theater.

But my plan passed the acid test. It had me worried and impressed that it had no resistance at all. Never heard a negative word from The House or her lawyers.

JANUARY 9, 1970

Robin was my first treat one at a time weekends. She asked to take her best friend from JB, Linda, she considered Linda a sister, along with us. So damned much better. A really nice, fun time for them and a quiet, restful time for me ... for a change.

At three-thirty the following Friday, I was parked in front of the school when Robin and her closest friend, Linda, from their time together at JB, load into our rig with their gear for the weekend.

Robin introduced Linda. "Dad, this is my dear best friend, Linda." to her, "Linda, this is my dad."

I kidded Robin with, "But, I always thought that I was your best friend?"

She slugged me and then grabbed a hug.

The girls opted for a Taco Bell dinner which was my first time trying that outfit. Hmmm. Worked well. We went to the kid's movie, *Pippi* which they really enjoyed.

Then I found a hook-up park just off the beach in Santa Monica for the night.

Saturday, we spent the entire day at the Ocean Park Amusement Center. Costly, but worth it.

Sunday, much, much cheaper by spending the day at the beach just north of Malibu, Zuma Beach. Tough time there. Had to take the long way drive around since the rig was too tall for the shortcut underpass under Highway One.

McDonald's got the farewell dinner vote. We then dropped Linda off where I met her mother as the girls had excitedly told her about their most wonderful weekend.

Back in front of 144, we had trouble. She gave me a warm hug with, "Do I have to go?"

"The law says, yes."

Sobbing, "You have no idea what's ...."

Holding her tightly, "Please ... please Honey, I don't want to cry now. Please, just ...."

She bolted out the door, leaving it open as she dashed into the house.

JANUARY 6, 1970,
MEETING IN
LOYD'S OFFICE

In Loyd's One Wilshire conference room, Jackie, her attorney Sid Kahn with an accountant from Singer, Lewak, Greenbaum and Goldstein sit on one side of the long table as Loyd and I entered, to take the opposite side of the table.

Loyd greeted each of the opponents while I just took a seat quietly. This is the first time I've seen Jackie and I had lost fifty pounds making me look quite gaunt, and had shaved since the first few weeks of our marriage. Jackie had a slight reaction to my different appearance.

Loyd opened with, "Good afternoon."

Khan and the accountant rose and shook Loyd's offered hand.

Indicating Jackie, Kahn says, "Loyd, I'd like you to meet Missus Ward."

Loyd just nodded and, "How do you do, Missus Ward." They all sat.

Loyd, addressed Kahn, "Sid, I'd like your permission to address your client directly."

With a slight head nod, "Within reason, go ahead." Loyd faced Jackie and smiled, "May I call you Jackie?" She darted a look of questioning to Kahn who nodded 'yes' to her.

She then just nodded her consent.

Nodding back, "Thank you." A big slow deep breath and, "Well, Jackie, you must be aware that David has no desire for this divorce. He feels that you can fix whatever is wrong between the two of you with some outside help like marriage counseling. I prefer to see such a fine family, with no history of any of the usual irreconcilable problems many couples we see in court every day."

He just stared for some sign of recognition. "I must ask you for a verbal response to my question about having professional help to save your marriage."

Kahn jumped in with, "I think I can answer for my client. She has no interest in counseling of any sort."

Quite a big silence. Loyd just stared at Jackie for a long moment. Then, he referred to his folder before him on the table and turned to me.

"David, please confirm my notes. All of these children are yours with your wife?"

Slowly, "Yes."

"Douglas Kevin Miles is now six?" I nodded 'yes.'

"Dennis Keith Perry is now nine?"

With a look of question, I again, nodded 'yes.' "David Kirk Louis is now eleven?"

Now I'm getting antsy. 'Yes'

"And Jon Robin is now thirteen and on her next birthday she will be fourteen?"

I'm so lost I don't reply to this question.

"Again, Jon Robin will be fourteen next June 5th ... 1970?"

"Well, yes ... sure ... but...."

Kahn has caught the gist of Loyd's questions and vaulted up with, "This meeting is over." to Jackie, "Jackie, we'll have to have a private meeting. I know where Mister Saunders is going, and we're just not prepared."

Now standing, Loyd offers, "I would suggest that when you meet with your client you might highly suggest a private meeting between our clients."

Visibly shaken, Kahn replies, almost snidely, "I will surely take that proposal under advisement."

Kahn signals the accountant to fold his folder, took Jackie's arm to get her onto her feet.

I just stayed seated because I'm totally lost in this meeting falling apart at what was supposed to be a major legal processing event.

To the accountant, Kahn patted his shoulder with, "Thanks for coming in. We'll call Mister Greenbaum later." Back to Jackie, picking up his now closed and zipped briefcase, "Let's get some coffee."

And as they all leave, Loyd called out, "Be sure to get your parking validated. See Teri outside, as you leave."

I'm in total confusion as we are now moved back into Loyd's office. As he hung his coat on the back of his chair, I flopped into my usual chair in a complete loss about what just happened in that conference room.

I blurted out "Okay, what the hell was that all about? Here I am ready to fight over a settlement and they walk out."

Slowly finishing lighting, a new cigar, while smiling, "Just another legal trick. Did you see how quickly Sid caught on?"

"Caught on to what? Can I get in on the reason for the big sheepish grin painted all over your face?"

As he plopped into his chair, blowing smoke upward, "The minute I asked you when Robin's fourteenth birthday was, Sid folded. I'll bet quite a bunch that he and Jackie are, right now, down in the One Wilshire Coffee Shop and he's explaining the real facts of this case to her. Didn't you say she told her sister that 'David will never fight me.'"

"Yes, but..."

As he puts the cigar into the ashtray, "Well, Sid is now telling her the awful truth about divorce. What kind of fight she's really into. Now ... NOW, we'll file a request with the court for a reconciliation hearing which they will refuse but will put us on record of trying and adding another negative to their balance sheet when we eventually get into court."

Later that afternoon, back in my mother's living room with Ginny, having explained to the totally unexpected way the greatly feared day went, the telephone rang. Mother moved into her den and answered. "Hello." She listened a moment, the, "Yes, just a moment."

She slowly covered the phone and called to me, "It sounds like Jackie. Are you here?"

I just shook my head, rose and moved to the phone, "Hello," and listened. "I guess so ... wait a minute." I covered the mouthpiece and asked Mother, "Mother, can I borrow your car? Jackie wants to get together for a bite to eat."

I pulled the Chrysler onto our Van Ness parking pad next to the Wagon. I got out, approached the front door and reached for the doorbell button. Before I could push it, the front door opened, and with a few polite 'hellos,' we crossed to the Chrysler, and I held the door open for her to get in.

We drove west, silently, along Beverly Boulevard. Finally, I asked her, "Where would you like to eat?"

Obviously up so tight, she came out with, "I really can't eat. Can we just talk?" "Where?"

"Just park somewhere ... anywhere."

I pulled an immediate left off Beverly onto Lucerne and pulled over to park and quietly waited for her opening.

Finally, "David, I need to discuss the future of the children ... what's best for them ... for their future." a long silence while she reloaded her nerves. "I think it is most important that the children stay together ... not disrupt the ...."

Quietly fuming, "What in hell do you think their lives haven't been blown all to hell in the past six weeks? You've gotten rid of Ruth, brought your mother into their home ... and I know they're most unhappy with that. Talk about screwing up their normal family routine."

Now, talking to her closed window so I can't see her face, "I just think that they would all be better off in the home that I can provide."

"Aw, come on, Jackie. Lately you're gone most of each day. Ruth and I handle most of their daily problems. And, as you've said so many times over in the past years, 'you are so much better with the kids than I am. I should just have had the kids and let you raise them.'"

Now looking toward the front car window, "There have been times when you had your office on Vine, with George and Roger, when you were gone quite a lot." "Only when I had a job. Otherwise, I was home. And I worked at home a lot unless I had to have a big crew."

She started to look at me, but then went back to her window. "I wish you wouldn't fight me on this."

Shaking my head ever so slowly, "My God, I'm sure you would. My offer still stands. If you'll go to a counselor of some sort, someone we both agree on like Paul Richlie or a minister or whatever, I'll walk away and not contest you."

A huge deep breath and, "I just can't do that."

"You can do anything if your stupid pride doesn't get in your way." A big sigh, and "Jackie, you may have the cards stacked against me, but out of those fifty-two cards, I have the four aces ... Robin, Kirk, Keith and Kevin."

She looks away but can't allow herself to cry.

FRIDAY JANUARY 16, 1970, KIRK'S FIRST WEEKEND

Now it was Kirk's turn with me for a weekend. For his choice he wanted to take the brand-new red Honda 90 minibike Jackie bought him with us on the front of the Beechwood. It replaced the homemade Taco I'd taken on our fabulous trip around the country last July.

We decided to go into the Lake Elsinore area with its quite rural surroundings.

I found a KOA Camp later that night where we hooked the rig up. Early Saturday morning, after breakfast, we unloaded the shiny, stock Honda and Kirk started riding when the park manager stopped us with, "Sorry guys, no riding motors within the park. Bicycles are okay. Motor bikes ... no."

I apologized with, "Sorry. Didn't know ...."

"Quite understandable. Happens quite often." After a second thought he continued with, "Hey, there's a really great area back in that canyon ..." he pointed off towards the mountains and "... over there. Lots of motors there. They even race on Saturdays. All classes and ages of riders."

With that info, we reloaded the Honda on the front rack, and we quite easily found our way into the foothills draw where the Lake Elsinore Motor Sports Park was with its motocross track and riding trails all throughout the surrounding hills and small valleys.

I was thrilled to see, for the first time since the bomb destroyed our family life, Kirk was so happy, smiling, and enthused. It was hard to keep him off the bike. Even lunch was a very fast gulp. Thankfully I had an extra five-gallon fuel can and that the Honda had a four-stroke engine.

At sunset the lights turned on and the track is cleared. Kirk pulled up next to the rig, switched his engine off and entered to join me. I'd been working on one of my screenplays which made the day great for both of us.

"Hey Dad, they said they had to clear the track for the races tonight. Seems every class of bikes race ... even minibikes. Can we stay and watch the races? We have our own food. Can we, please ... please?"

"This was the beginning of a life changing experience. Watching the two events which had boys about Kirk's age out there on different horse-power bikes was the best thing that brought us all together as a family."

FRIDAY JANUARY 23

The following weekend was nine-year-old Keith's choice. He sat in the co-pilot's seat as we were on our way to Santa Barbara. "This is great Dad. We're real heavy into studying the Missions of California and I'll be able to write a real report of what we'll really find."

"Glad this helps with you getting personal information firsthand."

A few more miles of idle conversation when I broke the calm with, "Hey, we know they're closed until morning." I check Keith out, "what about pulling over and spend the night here and start out ...?"

"Sure. Get some rest and have a snack?"

Right now, we were on State Highway101just lowering down out of the foothills about twenty miles south of Ventura when I pulled the Beechwood off 101 and into a deserted cul-de-sac about two hundred yards from the highway. We fixed and had dinner while discussing what he hoped to learn about both the Ventura and Santa Barbara missions that none of his classmates are lucky enough to discover.

Setting up for sleeping, he asked me, "Dad, do you talk with or see much of Ruth? We all sure miss her. Such a lonely home without her."

Slowly, "well, sure. Actually, I see her often. We've been doing some fascinating psychic experiments. Had no idea ... all those years living with her, that she was such a psychic person."

Now totally involved, "Really? Gosh." A deep quiet and then, slowly, "What are you ...?"

"We've been making contacts with what truly seem to be high level spirits and ...."

Completely into it now, "Dad, could we please go visit Ruth? Right away? I really miss her."

Checking my watch, I saw it was almost eight-fifteen. "Let's ready the rig to travel. It's still early."

Quick action stowing things, then we were back on the 101 now heading south, towards Ruth, instead of north.

All I remember is that it was a great weekend for us both.

FEBRUARY 14, 1970,
MOVING BACK HOME

Finally, it was about nine o'clock on Valentine's night when I opened the driveway gates at 144 N. Van Ness Avenue and backed the rig in, just behind the gates, allowing room for the Pontiac to back off the pad in front. I closed the gates and began moving my gear back into my garage studio.

Well, it took from August twenty-fifth, nineteen sixty-nine until tonight, February fourteenth, nineteen-seventy ... that's one hundred and eighty days before I finally took Paul's, Roger's and Loyd's wise advice and moved back into my home."

A bit of backstory here:

I'd removed my very old, original two car garage and replaced it with a two story, 24 by 36-foot-wide building. The upper floor was designed for my office with the capabilities of all night working, which happens quite often. Forty hours of work happened about every two weeks or so. A complete tiny bathroom and small kitchenette area also. It could also sustain having a crew of copyists there and not in the house anymore.

The added length to the lower garage area I'd designed for all my woodworking tools easily in front of the cars ... which were always parked on the pad in front.

For some never learned reason, after the shocking separation, I guess Jackie's advisors had the final inspection during which, the shower became illegal. What I later laughed about for the longest time was that I had the signed-off bathroom permit where the shower had been approved. Later situations make this error on their part quite obvious.

This shower-less bathroom then caused me to, in my bathrobe and with a towel over my arm go down to the back slider into the family room, knock on and get Beatta to open it so I could use Ruth's shower in that bathroom. (I would wonder what the neighbors thought of that scene?)

The backstory ended now: That Saturday night I unloaded my food stuffs into the small refer and put some supplies in the small pantry closet area. Then, with only my sleeping bag and a large pillow I fought trying to fit my six foot-three body onto the six-foot sofa to fitfully sleep.

Sunday morning, the kids, seeing the rig in the driveway and guessing I was home, they came roaring past the pool and up the balcony stairs with tears.

After about an hour of excitement, taking turns venting their/our joy, the back slider of the house opened and Beatta stepped onto the deck and called, "Children, come on. We're ready to go."

I asked, "Where ...?"

Robin piped in with, "Mom's taking us to Disneyland." Moving toward my slider, Kevin threw in, "Yep!" Beatta again, "Come on. Your Mother's waiting."

I moved them toward the door with, "Can't keep Walt Disney waiting. He needs the money." Ad Libs of, "Oh, Dad, come on, Dad," etc.

The five of us left the studio, crossed past the pool, up the three steps and in through the slider into the family room.

Jackie and Beatta were there, ready to leave.

Jackie moved to the slider, "David, we are ready to leave, and I have to lock up."

I got a huge flash and replied, "Go ahead. I'll lock up when I leave."

Beatta looked to Jackie for her answer. The kids watched the scene. I didn't move.

After a very tense moment, Jackie folded with, "Come on, kids, let's go." The children looked back at me as the party left through the front door.

I stood on the front stoop as the wagon loaded, backed off the pad and drove off.

I then re-entered my empty home, closed the front door after trying my old key in the door to learn the lock's been changed.

Curious about anything of mine still remaining in our master bedroom, I climbed the stairs, crossed the landing to the bedroom door. A dead bolt stopped the door from opening.

I tried the knob twice, I smiled, then returned down three steps on the stairs, I stopped and looked back at the locked bedroom door. After a moment of contemplation, humming loudly, I re-crossed the landing and without stopping, shouldered the door open—just like in the movies. I slowly walked through the room looking for evidence of my belongings. Seeing nothing obvious, I opened what had been my top dresser door. Only feminine wear. Then I discovered a second private telephone instrument sitting side by side with the original house line on her nightstand.

I left the bedroom, closed the shattered jamb door, down the stairs, to check the front door lock. I then went into the kitchen tool drawer to get one of my screwdrivers to remove the front door lock as well as the back slider lock.

Then, on my Honda 90 to a Western Avenue locksmith to re-key both doors with an extra set of keys for Jackie. To hell with Beatta.

I then re-installed the newly keyed locks, and I left the front door unlocked for the family's return entry. The new keys for both doors I placed on the kitchen counter.

In the early evening the family returned. Jackie, seeing the partially smashed bedroom door, rushed to buy a Polaroid camera to take pictures for evidence of violence, in court.

MARCH 12, 1970

On March 12th, we finally had our first court date with Judge Cox, where the temporary order for joint custody was ordered.

I slowly paced the Superior Court Hall silently reciting the 23rd Psalm as told to by Kate. Ruth sat on a hallway bench, waiting when Barry and Sharon surprised us as they exited the court's doors, seeing Ruth first they go over to her with hugs.

I moved in behind them, tapping both shoulders. They turned and I asked, "Oh, my God, what the hell are you two doing here? What's ...?"

Nonsmiling and extremely serious, Barry answered with, "Judge Alexander asked us both to come in to have a talk with him."

Sharon reached out touching my arm, "He told us not to talk with anyone about it. No one." She gestured zipping up her mouth.

Shaking his head at her action, Barry, emphasizing what she'd just said, "He was very serious about that."

"Okay, okay," I stammered, "Does Loyd know about ...?"

Shaking his head, Barry can only say, "Sorry. Can't comment. The Judge was dead serious about that."

Squeezing my arm harder, "Yes, Uncle Bidu, Barry's right. The Judge was dead serious ... and almost threatening."

After a silent moment to let that statement settle in, "I understand." I looked toward the court doors, "Is Loyd in there?"

Slowly shaking his head, "Didn't see him. Just the judge."

I reached out to touch both of them, and with a group hug I said, "Thanks, guys. Talk to you later."

I turned and went through the court doors while Ruth looked after me with a confused look when joined by Sharon and Barry.

Later I came to find out that this meeting was called because Robin had told a counselor that she didn't want to live with either parent. When asked to choose a place to live she opted for living with Barry and Sharon. That spoke highly of her resentment for the divorce ... as I now interpret the meaning behind that event. At least I learned how far the court would go to ensure the stability of the children. Thank God for that protection."

A few days later a sheriff officer served me papers at the studio door while Beatta peeked out the slider from the family room.

I had no problem accepting the service.

Really can't remember how many days it was after the broken bedroom door event happened, but there's a knock on my glass slider which I answered. A telephone serviceman stands there with his toolbox in hand.

I opened the door. And asked, "Yes?" "Sir, I'm here to remove the two phones." "Really?"

"I have the order right here."

He produces an order, so I usher him in, pointing to my desk with one phone. As he moves toward the desk, "There are two lines up here, correct?" "Right. Hollywood 46---- and -----."

"Ah, that's what I'm after." and starts disconnecting the two phone lines. Thinking slowly, I asked, "Who ordered this?"

He stops, picks up the order and checks it with, "The order says, Missus Jacqueline Ward by a Sid Khan."

Musing softly, aloud, "Very interesting." a moment of thought and, "How can Sid Khan have anything to do with our phones?"

As he continues working, "Only the legal registered owner of the service can authorize any changes in service."

I asked another question, "Okay, who is the legal registered owner of this service?"

He stopped again, picked up the work order and comes up with, "Let's see, a David Ward is the ...."

Quietly thrilled, "Well, sir, I'm David Ward and I did not order any change in this/my service."

He's taken aback. "Do you have some way of identifying yourself, Mister Ward? "Hmmm, will my passport do? Or my driver's license?"

Since that first weekend with Kirk and experiencing Lake Elsinore Raceway, for three or four straight weekends, with all four kids now, we went back to Elsinore and even entered the three horse Taco for Keith and Kirk's Honda to try racing. Great fun but obviously far out classed bikes.

Those kid's dads had built the most powerful four to seven horsepower engines imaginable. Four foot seven Jeff Ward—later to become World's AAA Motocross Champion—raced there, sponsored by Bonanza Motors. We've just gotta do something. The second weekend we met Bob Grandberg. His son, Mark, had a very hyped bike. Bob then guided me into the ways of souping up minibike engines.

Kirk at the start of a race

Since Jackie kept the wagon parked on the front house pad, I had plenty of area to work, building and modifying bike motors and suspension in the new garage. I started with the old Taco. That was too stock. As each of the kids got home from school, almost every day, they headed straight for the garage for a progress report.

Then Saddleback Park out in the Lake Forrest area of Orange County was introduced to us as well as Indian Dunes just off I-5 in the Valencia area.

At Indian Dunes, was where Kirk, Keith and Robin, raced against Steve McQueen's daughter, Terry, and son, Chad, along with other minis from all over.

Robin raced in Powder Puff races against Terry and six other girls. This release of tension for us all made the following seventeen months of sitting on the legal fence much, much easier to survive.

Much of McQueen's huge hit movie "On Any Sunday" was filmed at those locations. Steve even brought World Champion Trials and Crossed Country champion Malcolm Smith out to The Dunes several times. He was a fascinating story all by himself.

Once Malcolm rode a light weight 125 up the 10" trunk of a tree until the bike lost traction and he slowly backed it down and rode off.

Having been the Baja 500 and 1,000 desert bike race champion several times, a really great story he told us about bikes was, "Leave the motor stock. Much more reliable on long hard runs. The suspension is what needs all the attention. Riding those rough desert sandy trails, you want the softest and most dependable ride you can get. A human body takes one hell of a lot of abuse on those runs."

Every afternoon, after school hours, the five of us, both in my studio and down by the pool, had fun until Beatta announced dinner, which ended those great moments together.

It took about a week after finally settling back into my temporary home address, when one afternoon, my mother's singing student, Virginia, after hearing my Mother's version of my traumatic happenings, called to reiterate what she'd gotten from her friend, Kate—a very psychic lady—into the action to help by calling me almost daily.

This emotionally fascinating help went on for over a week until I realized that, this unknown woman, to me, Kate, had what was happening to me so clear with her information she was passing on, that I got the feeling that Mother has joined in by adding her ideas into the information that Virginia was forwarding to me through Kate

A few days more of fun and Bob Barker's The Price Is Right mornings, when my phone rang. Answering with, "Hello?"

The as yet unfamiliar voice of Kate Porter said, "Hello? Is this David?" "Well, yes this is."

"David, this is Kate, Virginia's friend. You know about ...?"

"Well hell yes. Why ...?"

"David, I got the feeling that Virginia was not totally telling you what I said without adding ...."

"Are you serious? Wow! This has bothered me for over a week now."

Softly she asked, "Would you mind if I gave out my phone number so we can talk direct and ...."

Almost in shock, "Oh, my God, may I please ... don't want to overload your daily ...."

"David, please be sure, anytime ... I'm here for you, any hour. I have extremely deep feeling for what you and your wonderful family are suffering through."

One of those lousy days, unannounced, Jackie came up the pool side stairs, knocked on the slider, which I opened. She entered while quickly taking in the surroundings of how I was existing.

How, what her reason for this visit, I have no memory. The most important thing to recall was she was sitting on my short bed-couch while I was sitting in a chair across the coffee table separating us.

On my easel, standing by the far wall, there was a sketch I'd drawn some days ago. She kept looking at it while and looking back at it several times while we talked about what I had no idea.

Finally, she couldn't hold back anymore, she asked, "David, isn't that Kevin on that easel over there? Who dr ...?"

Without turning, "I did." Got the feeling that she was impressed.

Again, the timing and spacing were totally forgotten and not retrievable when I was talking, on the phone, with Dear Ruth about the way Kate had slowly evolved into this horrible Ward-family tragedy, through Mother and Virginia.

One morning Ruth had called. That's when I told her, "And ... hey, did I tell you about one of mother's pupils, a six foot tall black woman, Virginia, who has been in contact with a tremendously informed psychic friend of hers named Kate about this mess. I've had some really interesting thoughts and info on Jackie and her confused thinking right now.

A very slow dead pause and, finally, she opens up with, "No ... no, you haven't ... well, well, well," a long stare, into ...? And she finally blurts out "I might as well fess up and tell you, I've been getting all sorts of psychic messages about this mess, for several months now."

A great pause of reflections on my part, for her confession to sink in, while I reflected back over our history in our two different family rooms, at our ranch, and so many elsewhere during those great years together as our family.

"You? You never ... in all those, those ...?"

Quietly, while trying to bring me up to today in our long relationship, "Never had a need to tell you." A sob, "now, oh my God how, now I need to ... gotta stop this mess." A large throat clearing sound and, "Damnit, there's no ... not any reason except that she's flipped ... totally lost it. Listening to ...."

"Hey, Dear One, your many years with us sure ...."

A sniffle and, "That's what I can't get. That lady needs you more than anything in her life. You brought her up. The only negative I ever saw was when Janice dumped her 17-year-old brother Bobby on us. After weeks of hell, I had to finally throw him out."

"Those were really tough weeks. Our kids were secondary to Bobby's space. Really tough on the family ... and me, having to keep Jackie as close to calm as possible while juggling all those different scenes and emotions."

"Never understood, Jackie giving him Robin's bedroom where he did his drugs and things was a real slap for all of us."

"Did I ever thank you for grabbing command and cleaning that turd up?"

Now, along with Kate in almost daily phone contact, Ruth was another much-appreciated support call. When any of the kids were up with me, they had many, many fun and emotional moments talking with her.

After some weeks of rough weather through March and into April, the almost daily phone talks with Ruth prompted her to suggest that I make it out to her place, in the Watts area, where we can experiment with psychic readings and such fun events.

"Sure! Are you still out in the bungalow on the next lot behind Marge and Joe's ... squeezing through that gap between the fence and the garage?

"You got it. Same place for Stephanie and me."

Figuring out that trip, I said, "It's a bit over twenty miles from Van Ness through L.A, night traffic, in the dark. Prefer not to use the Beech with her eight miles to the gallon cost. My Honda 90 gets over sixty per tankful." A hearty guffaw, Loyd won't let me buy any other wheels. "Khan would just take them away from you, he said."

So, wearing my heavy-hooded wind breaker, I made that ride two or three times a week, over to Western and Third, right south a few miles and then east to Vermont Avenue for the long ride south, down to Century Blvd east, left and past what would finally become the 110 freeway and into Watts. This routine happened until Ruth was informed that she was needed to testify.

Her main gift and power was controlled on her Ouija board. Just the normal board, nothing different, we each had tender fingers of our left hands on the planchette. This allowed me to make notes in a large binder, situated with inches of the right ride of my board placement.

Well into our fourth or fifth month of these awe-inspiring sessions, on occasion I began feeling uneasy late into a session. I felt a presence. I'd quickly turn my head to search the darkened area of her living room. Thought I'd caught a glimpse of something or someone.

I finally had to ask her, "Hey Ruth, for the past month or so I'm getting heavier and heavier feelings—impressions that we're not here alone. Do you ev ...."

She leaned away from the board and studied my question for a moment. "That's really interesting ... you're feeling Phillip's presence." She gets up and gets a glass of water from the sink and comes back to stand over the table and board.

"Hmm, well ... he's been here quite a bit lately. Our situation has him really trying to help ... by finding out information we can't find by ourselves."

The ledger I'd been creating these past months must have had over one hundred and fifty pages. Pages so fascinating and reassuring about so many of life's questions, I still shudder when straining to remember one peek at a solution which was life changing.

As our legal processing became much more active, court ordered psychiatrist meetings, a few short court sessions, when Ruth realized that she was going to be forced to appear as a character witness, one night her late call interrupted my Johnny Carson Late Show with, "David ... now listen to me carefully, David, very, very carefully," Her tone made me aware that what she was about to say was ultra-serious. "You've got to destroy all of our psychic pages ... every last one."

Almost stunned while her words tried to sink in and make some sense for me, "Okay ... okay, damn it, what in hell are you saying? Destroy the greatest pages I've ever seen? Been able to touch? To re-read so many of the most outstanding thoughts I could ever imagine ... in words?"

As I began heated pacing, time seemed to stand still while she was letting me slow down enough to be reachable.

"David ... dear David ... if Jackie's lawyers ever knew got wind of those pages, they'd have you declared mentally unbalanced and incompetent to be with your children."

Stuttering, "But, all that ...."

"Believe me, please believe me, if they ever got hold of those pages .... Believe me. I've been warned."

After much heated pacing the studio, and re-reading those outstanding pages far into the night and a short nap, about 05:30 I got my paper cutter and cut those well over a hundred pages into strips. I then flushed those once-in-a-life words down the toilet. I fought back the tears to avoid crying as I sank onto my couch, emotionally spent. Small tears welled and took me over.

NOVEMBER 1970,
JIM CONS ME

This was my new usual morning. After my toasted English muffin with peanut butter and blackberry jelly added, chewed with milk sips topped off with my instant coffee, laced with half and half and at least two or more sugars—hang over from my very early years when my mother set my over-sweet coffee habit up to haunt me ever since. I'm now watching Regis & Katie Lee on TV when my phone rings.

Putting my almost-finished coffee mug down, I moved to my desk and picked up the receiver to answer.

"Oh, hi Jim. Long ti ....", I listened.

"Gaining strength, a little more down every day."

More listens.

"Gee, Jim, I haven't got the mental strength to tackle a ... too much legal shit falling every few days ... at least once a week."

He continued his pitch.

Shaking my head, with a slight snicker, "Well, losing over fifty-five pounds in just over a month really beat me up. People don't believe me, but I've learned ... the hard way sometimes, to not care what people who don't know the real story say."

(I listened.)

"You serious? I've never ..." (listening)

"Really?" (listening)

"Only one arrangement ... with three days to ... when's the date?" As I paced back and forth, the dialogue faded.

Finally hanging up after that very long hyped conversation, I slowly take my main music note-making-pen out of its rack and slowly examined the damage I did to it when I jammed it into my desk after finishing that last cue for the Stu Phillips film on that fatal August day.

I carefully assayed the bent custom built, by me, nib points totally not close together. After many moments of surveying the damage, I took the nib apart with my special Esterbrook pen tools into its three (two custom) parts. I then retrieved a small set of pliers from my middle desk drawer and started bending the nibs back, as close as I could without breaking either of them. Then re-grinding the stressed nibs to a smooth point. They show deep scars of metal abuse.

Filling the pen barrel with my custom-made India ink and trying the re-built nib out, I called Jim back with, "okay, I'll try it, if you will. I should know within an hour if it'll work."

About 16:00 that afternoon, Barbara Haskell, Jimmie's wife, delivered me a score up into my garage studio, knowing the route.

Looking around at the room setup, pointing at the couch, she, with great questioning horror, asks, "You mean you sleep on that? You're at least ...."

"Six foot three on a six-foot couch. That six feet includes the two arm rests ... so ...."

"My God, how in hell can ...?"

"I average two to three hours a night ... in my old sleeping bag.

"After she left. I started slowly copying the score late into night, with the Johnny Carson Show as my only company late at night.

That first score of Jimmie's got me back into making a living.

JANUARY 22, 1971,
BACK IN COURT

After a grueling tense morning session, when the court lunch break came, and Loyd hauled me into the lawyer's lounge where Esther had just delivered his brown bag lunch. While eating he chewed me out.

"Okay, David, this morning's session was a disaster. What the hell were you trying to do, give all the months of hard work away?"

As the one o'clock the afternoon court session had begun and I was back on the stand, one of her lead attorneys, Roger Stern, hammered on me with, "Mister Ward, this morning you spoke of the many conversations you've had with your four children since this petition began."

I just nodded "yes."

Stern turned to the court reporter and instructed with, "Let the records show that Mister Ward answered 'yes' to my question."

Back at me, "Will you please tell the court the subjects of those conversations?"

A long pause

I finally answered, "No!"

Stern looked at Loyd. "Mister Saunders, would you please advise your client that he will be in contempt of court if he refuses to answer my direct question?"

Loyd just smiled and shrugged.

Stern then turned to Judge Alexander. "Your honor, please advise the witness what his jeopardy is for not answering my question."

A thoughtful moment until the judge said, "Mister Stern, I can see no benefit in Mister Ward's answers on this matter today. Please go on with other questions."

Stern crossed to his desk and checked his notes.

Irritatingly hopeless, I was excused, and Jackie was called to face Loyd. She looked a bit nervous while Loyd was calmly checking his notes.

With notes in hand, he turned to her with, "Now, missus Ward, to continue, did you know or meet Jimmie Haskell in the last part of 1954?"

"Well, no."

"Johnny Mandel?"

"No, I ...."

He hurled in rapid succession, "Hoyt Curtin? Bob Thompson? Charles Stern?"

Stern rises for some point. "We stipulate that Missus Ward met those persons sometime after her wedding to Mister Ward."

As Stern sat down, she added, Jimmie Haskell did play music at our wedding reception ... on his accordion."

With a strange questioning look, "Your request? Your business connection?" Now becoming flustered, "Well, no. He and my husband ...."

He interrupted her with, "Thank you" and turned around and checked his notes. Then turned back to her with, "Then might I gather that these clients of your husbands were to become amongst your biggest clients after your wedding?"

After the session closed, Loyd and I walked out of the court room.

"Sir, I've admonished you before that we never discuss the case in the men's room or on elevators because attorney's plant eavesdroppers. This is different. What a difference between the morning session and this afternoon. You were brilliant and I want everyone to hear that."

The five of us went mini racing almost every weekend.

FEBRUARY 9, 1971

Just as the sun was starting the new day, at 06:01, a 6.5 earthquake in the Sylmar area hit the entire southland area.

I jumped out of my sleeping bag and stood in the doorway of the studio while watching below as the waves in our pool started swaying back and forth, the length of the pool. They gained momentum with each surge, finally thrashing out and up against the house. Up those three brick steps and against the glass slider of the Family room.

A bit after 09:00, I took my four children, touring the Sylmar area, surveying the devastating damage. We saw where the I-5 and Newhall freeway interchanges had collapsed shutting both those freeways down. We also saw the huge water reservoir held back by the Van Norman Dam which was in fear of collapsing. The huge population below the dam was evacuated as that fear grew.

APRIL 5, 1971, THE OFFER

"I'm pacing the hall quietly repeating the Twenty-Third Psalm per Kate's orders while waiting to start that day's nine o'clock hearing when the court doors burst open and Loyd rushed to me, grabbed both my shoulders with," David ... listen ... listen very, very carefully to me, David." He takes a very deep breath and, "They are offering you Robin and Kirk to ...."

Mentally stumbling, "Offering me what?"

"Carefully, David. Very slowly and carefully listen to my every word. We don't move from here until I know you understand and comprehend every word I'm saying."

I'm in almost complete shock as he mumbled inaudibly, now very slow with each word while lightly shaking my shoulders. "They are offering you your two oldest children, Robin, your daughter and your oldest son, Kirk. Jackie will keep Keith and Kevin living with her."

He studied me very carefully. "We have to get back in there right away. The Judge is waiting for your answer."

He pointed toward the court door. He started back inside, hauling me along, and I, in a complete daze trying to fathom the shock just being hit with, followed past the door Loyd is holding open and closes.

The following weeks later, the almost daily visit to Loyd's office for paper signings, I asked him what caused the Court to make that offer to give me two of my children? He answered, "The Judge was going to give you three. Only Kirk would stay with Jackie."

JULY 9, 1971

It was just after eight in the morning when my telephone rang. I lowered the TV volume and crossed to the desk and picked up the phone.

"Hello."

A charming female voice says, "Hi, I'm trying to reach a David Ward. This is the CBS Regis Philbin office calling.

"Hey, my favorite nine o'clock show."

"So nice to hear. I assume you're Mister Ward?"

"Yes."

"Thank you, Mister Ward. Mister Ward, Regis would like to talk with you, on air, this morning about ...."

Shocked, "With me?"

"Sir, haven't you seen this morning's papers?"

"Dear charming lady, I haven't seen a newspaper since August of nineteen sixty-nine. My daily history is, hopefully, surviving one day at a time for the last, many, many months. TV news is all I have."

"Gee ... well, Regis would like to interview you since your divorce has been so internationally explosive and ....

Questioningly, "Internationally?"

"At least London, Europe and ....

"Gee ... well ... gee, I'm sorry but this whole mess has been so traumatic that I've just been concentrating on surviving and taking care of the kids. I guess it must be some sort of a great story?" Long pause as I pace, holding the phone receiver. "It might be best to contact my sensational attorney, Loyd Saunders to talk to Regis."

"Thank you, Mister Ward. We will do that. And, thank you."

Fifteen minutes later after the usual opening banter and commercials of watching Regis and Kathy Lee, Regis had Loyd on the phone.

"Mister Saunders you and David Ward have created a male-saving situation here. I just wish I'd had you for my attorney when my marriage fell apart."

"Thank you, Regis."

It was about six that same day when I just happened to look out the front studio window to see our Wagon back off the pad and into the driveway. It then pulled out onto Van Ness. At the same moment, Robin and Kirk came into the studio.

A confused Robin said, "Dad, Mom says that since we now belong to you that she's taking Keith, Kevin and Grandma B to dinner and you have to feed us."

That shocking statement is greatly amplified by the lost look on both of their faces. Even more bewildered than they were, I looked toward my small kitchenette area with its microwave and refrigerator. I crossed to the refrigerator, opened its door and that of the small freezer area. There's only one frozen chicken pot pie in there and about a half of a quart of milk in the door slot.

Printed in the United States
by Baker & Taylor Publisher Services